Operati

Bill Tutte — Lorraine
Flowers
Computer

Operation Primrose:
U110, the *Bismarck* and the Enigma Code

David Boyle

Jointly published by Createspace and
THE REAL PRESS
www.therealpress.com

This edition published in 2015 by the Real Press,
Originally published as an ebook by Endeavour Press in 2015
www.therealpress.com

© David Boyle

ISBN 978-1517155810

For John Nicholson,
whose father appears in this book,
with love

Introduction

It was Winston Churchill who coined the phrase 'the Battle of the Atlantic'. "Amid the torrent of violent events one anxiety reigned supreme," he wrote later, "battles might be lost or won, enterprises might succeed or miscarry, territories might be gained or quitted, but dominating all our power to carry on the war, or even keep ourselves alive, lay our mastery of the ocean routes and the free approach an entry to our ports."

Even Churchill's rotund expressions and mastery of language fails to quite do justice to the reality in mid-Atlantic, as freighters, tankers and liners were sent to the bottom in fire and burning oil, protected by an exhausted and dwindling fleet of destroyers and escorts, while increasing proportions of our imports lay in the ocean depths, along with their crews. It was a story of grit, daring, and frustration on both sides, and of long, tiring nights on watch from the sea-swept bridge of a corvette or a damp, freezing conning tower.

Meanwhile, ten more ocean-going U-boats were completing every month by the end of 1940, and the British ports were filling slowly with damaged merchant vessels that could not be repaired. In desperation, at the start of 1941, Churchill wrote a memo to the First Lord of the Admiralty, A. V. Alexander, the minister responsible for the navy, warning that cargo ships arriving in the UK that month were half those which had arrived the same month in 1940.

"How willingly would I have exchanged a full-scale attempt at invasion for this shapeless, measureless peril, expressed in charts, curves and statistics," he wrote later.

This was the reality that lay behind the desperate efforts to crack the Nazi Enigma naval code. Bletchley Park, the top secret wartime cryptography establishment, had its own stresses – but all those involved in the struggle to crack naval Enigma knew the stakes.

**

The performance of Benedict Cumberbatch in *The Imitation Game*, and the fascination with the life and work – and the untimely death – of Alan Turing, has tended to throw the spotlight onto the extraordinary and secret work by these Bletchley Park code breakers. The narrative has concentrated on how the Enigma codes were cracked, and due respect has been given to all those aspects of the puzzle that came together – from the original Polish pioneers who helped to find ways of reading the early versions of Enigma and passed on their insights, and their Enigma machine, to the British, to the teams working around the clock in an obscure country house in the middle of Bedfordshire, from Turing's leaps of imagination and the beginnings of computing, to the inspirational contributions made by his colleagues which made the various steps possible.

By far the toughest aspect of cracking Enigma involved the complexities of the naval code. The army and Luftwaffe versions of Enigma succumbed to the code breakers relatively early and signals were read with increasing ease. But the naval versions still held out, for reasons that will be made clear in this short book.

The purpose of it is to tell a small slice of the story – the capture of a naval Enigma machine from U110 and its immediate consequences – but also to tell the tale in the context of one of the most important months in the business of cracking the naval Engima code, May 1941. That month saw both the capture of U110, together with an intact coding machine, just a few days after the first breakthrough – the capture of the naval Enigma settings for June – followed by the crescendo of the Battle of the Atlantic only days later: the pursuit and sinking of the German battleship *Bismarck*.

But the book has a secondary purpose. That is to try and set the story of the Enigma code-breakers at Bletchley Park back in the context from which it has been wrenched, the huge operation around naval intelligence which embedded Bletchley and the code cracking enthusiasts in Hut 8 in a wider machine that tried to use what clues were available to protect convoys, and read the minds of the enemy.

And perhaps most of all, the purpose is to set this story in the most important context of all: the fact that German code breakers had – even before the outbreak of war – been able to crack the British naval code and, while Turing and his collaborators were wrestling with the sophisticated Enigma system, their opposite numbers at B-Dienst in Berlin (until heavy bombing drove them out to the small village of Eberswalde) were reading most of the signals between the British Admiralty and its ships and convoys at sea.

This is not to diminish the achievements of the Bletchley people, which led to a series of individual victories from the Battle of Matapan to the Battle of North Cape, when the battlecruiser *Scharnhorst* was sunk. Harry Hinsley, who worked there himself – and wrote the definitive study of British intelligence in the Second World War – argued that cracking Enigma brought the war to an end at least a year sooner, because the U-boat threat had been comprehensively defeated at the start of 1944, allowing the necessary troops and material to be brought across the Atlantic to make D-Day possible.

There is no doubt about the crucial role that Bletchley played in the victory over the Nazis, and especially over the U-boats. But it is important to balance what we know of the bursts of individual brilliance with the systems and community effort of naval intelligence as a whole, and as it actually was – a day by day, hour by hour struggle by two sets of intelligence machines and, in particular, two sets of brilliant code breakers.

Part of the purpose of this book is to draw together that struggle when it reached its height, during that crucial month of May 1941 – when the very survival of Britain hung in the balance – to work out why one side managed by the skin of their teeth to develop the advantages that they could use eventually to defeat the other on the high seas.

2

"Silence that followed five minutes of continuous rapid firing so thick you could cut it with knife but it was gradually disturbed by distant indistinct droning from overhead high above in apparently empty sky of fleecy white clouds against blue ceiling of Mediterranean. The drone increased to buzz and suddenly changed to roar as squadron after squadron of speedy fighter planes and bombers were diving with motors full and broke through screen of white cloud and descended like swarm of bees not only on line British battleships but also on two cruisers carrying distinguished Egyptian guests... There's fifty thousand men and four hundred tons of steel clad dynamite waiting here with guns loaded and steam up and decks cleared for action. It's certainly going to be hell if it's ever turned loose."

The missing words reveal that this is a cable from an American newspaperman in Alexandria in the autumn of 1936, watching the end of the spectacular manoeuvres of the British Mediterranean Fleet under Admiral Sir William Fisher. It was a moment of triumph for the Royal Navy between the wars. It put aside the humiliations of the naval treaties, the Geddes Axe and other spending cuts, and the Invergordon Mutiny, and it demonstrated not just power but flair and showmanship.

Fisher himself didn't survive the following year – worn out by the administration of the coronation naval review at Spithead – or he would have been a similarly dramatic First Sea Lord during the war years. He had also, by his use of searchlights in these demonstrations of sea power, banished the memories of the Battle of Jutland, when he had commanded the battleship *St Vincent*, before the German High Seas Fleet had been allowed to escape by their superior night fighting abilities.

But that crucial moment of revival and international recognition in 1936 also marked a moment of disaster for the navy which would put it at a huge disadvantage in the war at sea when fighting broke out three years later. Because only a few months before Fisher's final manoeuvres, the circumstances had conspired to allow the navy's British wartime naval codes to be cracked by the other side. And Fisher's Mediterranean Fleet played its role in the disaster.

We have become so used to the picture of Alan Turing at Bletchley Park, cracking the Enigma code to win the Battle of the Atlantic, that we have tended to forget that, at the outbreak of war in 1939, the situation had been reversed. The Nazi Enigma code for the navy was completely opaque – though there were cracks already appearing in the army and Luftwaffe versions – yet the German navy were able to read most of the signals used by the British navy.

To understand why, you have to go back four years, to the summer before those spectacular manoeuvres by the Mediterranean Fleet, to the moment when the Italian dictator Benito Mussolini first threatened to build an Italian empire in Africa by invading Abyssinia.

The crisis had been building for most of the year, as Italian troops began mobilising on the borders of Abyssinia (modern Ethiopia), encouraged by an arms embargo on both sides imposed by the British and French that undermined Ethiopia's ability to resist. As the summer turned to autumn in 1935, the League of Nations struggled to prevent war. Mussolini crossed the border at the beginning of October.

In the weeks before that, a wider war in the Mediterranean seemed, if not exactly likely, then quite possible. The British navy scrambled to take up positions. Fearing a pre-emptive attack by the Italians on their fleet base in Malta, Fisher moved his ships rapidly to Alexandria. They also scrambled to find ways of speedily reinforcing the British naval units in Aden, a new British naval base in what is now Yemen, but which was at least close to the action.

The cruiser *Dunedin* dashed from New Zealand, *Norfolk* and the old cruiser *Emerald* came from Colombo to Aden, *Ajax* and *Exeter* from the West Indies to reinforce the fleet at Alexandria. The cruiser *Sussex* – another distinctive three-funnelled County-class cruiser, the workhorse of the fleet in the 1930s – made it all the way from China Station. Then came the destroyers: the Second Destroyer Flotilla, led by the destroyer leader *Kempenfelt,* made it through the Suez Canal from Egypt to support the others in Aden. All shore leave was cancelled, and remained cancelled until Mussolini marched into Addis Ababa in May.

The navy was ready for war with Italy. Fisher and his wife were arranging to have naval families evacuated from Malta, and there is no doubt that Fisher would have accomplished the ensuing action with his usual flair if war had come. But if it didn't, and as it began to seem unlikely, then the Abyssinian crisis was at least an opportunity to practice going onto a war footing. The ships in Aden, closest to the Italians, began using their wartime codes.

During normal operations, the Royal Navy used a five-digit cipher, which used five numbers to denote each letter or punctuation mark in a signal. For two decades now, the German code breaker Wilhelm Tranow had been studying this code and was able to use his detailed knowledge of British naval movements, and – when merchant ships were involved – use information gleaned from *Lloyd's Weekly Shipping Report,* to read most signals using this very basic cipher.

But in wartime, the British used a four-digit code as well, double coding their messages first with the wartime code and then with their usual five-digit cipher, and this is what they did in Aden in 1935. Their messages were then picked up in the Black Forest town of Villengen, in the far south of Germany, which for the previous decade had been the German navy's southernmost signal listening station.

The chance to pit their wits against the British naval code in wartime conditions was a huge opportunity for the cryptographer Wilhelm Tranow and his colleagues at the tiny cryptography service *Beobachtungsdienst,* known as B-Dienst. Once he realised what was happening, he and his team were able to strip the five-digit cipher off the code. The newspapers were reporting which naval units were in Aden and Alexandria. It was the only region where the code was being used in this way, and there were only a limited number of ships involved.

Even under the conditions of the Abyssinian crisis, and the small number of naval units in Aden, matching ships to code letters was hardly simple but, with Tranow's meticulous knowledge, it was possible.

The following summer, in 1936, there were British naval units off the coast of Spain, making up the international observation force for the Spanish Civil War. Again, this provided an opportunity to check the process. By the end of 1936, the Britain's wartime naval code had been well and truly cracked.

**

Tranow was unusual for a code-breaker. He was highly organised and a good manager. He was tall and erect and was then working as a civilian in the Kriegsmarine, the German navy, though he had served in the High Seas Fleet during the First World War as a naval telegraphist.

It was there that he first came to the notice of the naval authorities in 1914, and his skills failed to meet with their approval. He was a signals operator on the old battleship *Pommern*, when he received a copy of a badly coded message from the cruiser *Emden*. Bored and privy to the exchange, Tranow heard the flagship flash back that the message was unreadable and please would they re-code and re-transmit. On an impulse, he grabbed a pencil. After a little work, he had cracked the incorrect coded message and was able to save his colleagues on *Emden* the trouble by forwarding their decoded message to the flagship, in the correct code.

His superiors were horrified. To them, this looked like a serious and deliberate breach of security and Tranow was put under arrest, then – when the fuss had died down – he was banned from secret work. It was two years before his former colleague Lieutenant Commander Martin Braume had been plucked out of the German High Seas Fleet to set up a centre for code-breaking at Neumünster, and he asked for Tranow.

Tranow's career only ended temporarily when the war effort collapsed in 1918, but the code-breaking unit was reconstituted under Braume the following year and he was asked back. Throughout the great inflation, the violent political upheavals and the rise of Adolf Hitler in the 1920s and 1930s, Tranow remained in post, building his knowledge of his British counterparts, their ships, movements and call signs, and their habits and procedures. He hung on while the continued existence of B-Dienst and its code-breakers hung by threads. At one stage, they were all sent to Kiel to share offices with the torpedo and mines inspectorate.

In was only in 1934, with the arrival of the energetic and enterprising Commander Heinz Bonatz to take charge, that B-Dienst was back in business. By the outbreak of war, five years later, 500 code-breakers were working in their headquarters in Berlin, as part of the new Maritime Warfare Command. Soon there were 6,000 of them.

If Tranow was a professional, and he had been at work on these same problems almost continuously since 1916, his opposite number in the UK – overseeing the business of cracking the German naval code – was an amateur, in the best sense. Dillwyn (Dilly) Knox was a classical scholar, the son of an evangelical bishop of Manchester and had been deeply influenced by the Greek scholar Walter Headlam. His brother was the famous Roman Catholic convert Ronald Knox. At one stage in his career, he had tutored the future prime minister Harold Macmillan. He had been a friend of the economist John Maynard Keynes at Cambridge, who said he had a "powerfully confused brain", and at the same time had been the object of erotic desire for Lytton Strachey. He was extremely shy and, like Turing, rather gauche. So much so that, when he was younger, he had gained the nickname 'Erm…'

At the outbreak of war in 1939, Knox was 55 and was the chief cryptographer at Bletchley Park. He was known for his peculiar habit of reciting Milton's *Paradise Lost* while driving, letting go the steering wheel at moments of high emotion. He appeared to live on a diet exclusively comprised of chocolate and black coffee. It was his task to lead the charge against Enigma, which he managed using a system known as 'rodding', which allowed him to use a crib – a good guess at the meaning of one phrase in a coded signal – to deduce the settings of the first rotor of the Enigma machine. It was a system using logic and linguistics rather than mathematics.

Knox and Tranow may never have heard each other's names, but they were actually old adversaries. Knox had worked in the famous Room 40 at the Admiralty as a codebreaker during the First World War, and was largely responsible for the big breakthrough cracking the German naval code in 1916, the year that Tranow began his career as a professional. It was Knox who realised that one long signal seemed to repeat the same two letters at the end of every sentence, and suggested that it might be poetry. It turned out to be verses written by the great German poet Friedrich Schiller.

It was the turning point in the struggle to crack the German naval code, but it was to have a disadvantage too. The British Admiralty came to believe too strongly in their own superiority in cryptography. Given the resources, and the sense of national emergency, or so they tended to think, the enemy's codes could be cracked by their inherent ingenuity and the necessary intelligence would be forthcoming. It was a fatal mistake. They were not, of course, aware of Tranow's great success and that – at the outbreak of war – their own naval signals were being read, though with some delays, by their enemy. But they were only too aware of the huge problem posed by the Enigma naval code, which seemed not just difficult but probably uncrackable.

**

Enigma had been invented by the electrical engineer Arthur Scherbius, mainly for industrial security. It operated like a typewriter, so that the operator at one end typed in a letter and a different key would light up. These substitutes were noted down and the whole signal sent by morse code. At the other end, the telegraphist would simply input the message and the Enigma machine would reveal the original.

Inside the machine, there were three rotors (and later more than three) which could be arranged in different ways, each one linked to a different set of electrical connections. The key code, with the rotor setting, would be in a three letter key for each day, which all the machine operators would look up in the code book. It was believed to be impregnable. The three rotors could mean more than 17,000 different solutions for a given message, but – since the three rotors could be re-arranged in any of six different ways – the number of combinations reached well over that. In fact, with all the additions used by naval Enigma – the steckerboard, trigrams and bigrams – the possible permutations were calculated at one stage at 10^{104}.

Enigma had a few weaknesses, even so. One was that no letter was ever represented by itself. For another thing, the machine would have to go through all 26 positions before the middle rotor moved, which meant you knew that the first 26 letters of any message only used one rotor. There was also the fatal mistake made by the German military which was that the three letter key setting were usually sent twice and you knew there would be a link between the first and fourth letters and so on (this stopped in May 1940).

Knox and his colleagues at Bletchley Park, known in those days simply as Station X, were not quite starting from scratch. They could rely on the previous breakthroughs by the Polish mathematicians who had been able to read Enigma messages for some time, using the system's weaknesses. Led by the mathematicians Jerzy Rozycki, Henryk Zygalski and Marian Rejewski, they had used a system of paper with punched holes with all the possible combinations and shone lights through from below, shifting the papers around until one light shone all the way through. They called this system, and the machine that helped them, the *bombe*. It was to link up with Turing's own ideas about computing.

The German naval authorities had tried to use the army version of Enigma, but quickly realised they needed something else. The army needed machines that were portable and light. The navy had no need to worry about portability, but they were extremely nervous about the possibility that their codes could be compromised, so they developed a naval version. It had four rotors instead of three, with a bigger choice of possible rotors to use.

There were other safeguards. The code books which were published each month used a special ink and paper which were designed to dissolve on contact with sea water, though this caused other problems for U-boats in particular. It meant that submarines had to keep a duplicate set of messages somewhere in the control room or radio room because there was so much water splashing over the conning tower. They could hardly keep the paperwork in a special watertight bag because the whole point was that they should dissolve. This may have been one of the factors in the capture of so much Enigma paperwork in Operation Primrose.

There were other occasional clues. Sometimes radio operators would send their signals in plain text, then realise their mistake, apologise and start at the beginning again in code. But that kind of breakthrough happened only rarely. German weather flights made use of such a narrow range of signals that they were extremely useful for the production of Turing's cribs, so they were not molested – except, as we shall see, when more information might be revealed.

Otherwise, Knox and his colleagues feared that only a working Enigma machine, set up correctly and with the correct code settings would allow them to read the enemy's signals. That is certainly what the German navy believed. Knox's first encounter with a machine came in July 1939 when the Polish cryptographers realised that the number of basic Enigma rotors to choose from had changed from a choice of three to a choice of five, as they did in 1938. They decided they needed something more sophisticated than the prototype paper-based computer, and offered to share their progress with the British and French counterparts.

Knox and his commanding officer at Bletchley, Commander Alistair Denniston, went to Warsaw at the end of the month, for the second time, and were given a stolen Enigma machine. It was just five weeks before the outbreak of war. Knox was considered to have been irritable and jealous, or so Denniston claimed in his letter of apology, but they brought home the machine in triumph and in the strictest secrecy to Bletchley Park. The invasion of Poland and open war was by then only a month away.

Bletchley was itself something of an enigma. It was a large mock Tudor country house, deliberately chosen by the head of secret intelligence, Captain Quex Sinclair, because it was on the railway line midway between the two ancient university towns of Oxford and Cambridge. Throughout the war, under huge stress and some discomfort, the government's secret code-breakers lived in ever-greater numbers at Bletchley – until as many as 12,000 people worked there – and the captured code books and the occasional captured coding machine were rushed there, sometimes so fast from a crashed plane that the blood stains on the code book were still wet.

The mathematician Alan Turing arrived there in a small group, under the usual code of 'Captain Ridley's Shooting Party', on 4 September 1939. Around him were not just mathematicians and crossword experts, but linguists, statisticians, puzzle creators, and strange individuals from the future novelist Angus Wilson to the future Home Secretary Roy Jenkins, and the future historian Asa Briggs, all of them in their own enclosed huts, revealing nothing to the outside world and little to each other. There were Egyptologists, bridge players, even one expert on seaweeds and mosses who had been sent there because of a misunderstanding of the biological term 'cryptogams', and who played a critical role working out how to dry out code books damaged by sea water.

The historian Hugh Trevor Roper, who visited often, described the atmosphere as "friendly informality verging on apparent anarchy". One military policeman famously mistook Bletchley for a military asylum.

The staff at Bletchley worked 24 hours a day, kept deliberately ignorant of the big picture, and without knowing what the purpose was of the hut and sometimes the desk next door. It was an all-pervading secrecy drummed into them which lasted until the 1980s. There is one story of a married couple who met after war and each separately received an invitation to the Bletchley reunion, half a century on, without knowing that the other had worked there.

By the outbreak of war, the code breakers at Bletchley had some advantages. They were soon able to recognise the codes of origin for each message, and – despite the short supply of coloured pencils – they began to code them visually, yellow for the Norwegian campaign, green for the army, red for the Luftwaffe. This was the situation when Turing arrived there, and was given the task of overseeing the theoretical aspects of cracking the coded messages. He was soon known as 'The Prof'.

In the early weeks of the war, he spent his time writing out in an almost illegible longhand a plan for cracking the codes, working the whole process out logically. The key point was that Coded Enigma messages were reversible, and – since they were reversible – they could reverse the process which the machine went through. Turing believed they would need two elements. The first was a series of what he called *cribs*, bits of code that were likely-looking translations. The second was a much improved, much faster version of the Polish bombe – a machine for testing out the various cribs to see if they worked, without which the whole process would be impossibly time-consuming. Speed was always vital at Bletchley Park.

Likely phrases would be recognised in signals and put through their 'bombe' prototype computers until one of these 'cribs' revealed the settings which turned coded gibberish into comprehensible German. It was a system that they knew, thanks to Turing, as 'banburismus', after the origin of the big sheets of paer (Banbury). But to try that, they would need to decode the settings, which were separately turned into pairs of letters known as bigrams.

What Turing found was that there was one weakness in naval Enigma which is that, sometimes, the three letter indicators for the rotor settings changed half way through the message, and then stayed the same for the next message. You could recognise this by the number of times letters in the signal aligned with each other – if they aligned only one in 17 times, then the chances were that the settings overlapped; if not it was usually one in 26 (a random sequence). Turing's technique was to use long cards, pioneered in Poland but printed in Banbury – hence the name – with holes punched in them, which could compare two messages, looking for the light to show through the holes to see where they might overlap.

There were clues also because Enigma was 'reciprocal' – if A was represented by M then M was also represented by A. So it could then be possible to rule out various positions until the right hand rotor for the message had been identified, and so the process went on. It was possible to identify which rotor wheel was being used, because most of them used a different letter to turn over to the next wheel.

Then there were the problem of the cribs. There were clues. Sometimes it was clear that some messages were weather reports. Sometimes the words 'weather' or Heil Hitler!' were obvious. One signaller was in the habit of ending his signals 'nothing to report' (*nicht zu melden*). But it was Turing's colleague John Herival who provided the best route for cribs. He was dozing by the fire, and woke up with a start, imagining himself as a German signal officer with an Enigma machine, and suddenly realised that laziness would mean they would often just use the same settings as the day before. Straight away, he began to work out how to detect when they did.

Then there was the problem of a crib testing machine. This time, it was not enough to imagine the kind of computing machine that might solve the problem. Turing and his colleague Gordon Welchman (from Hut 6) had to actually build one. His first *bombe* was called Victory. It was seven feet long and six feet high, and it weighed a ton. It had the power to simulate the actions of 30 Enigma machines at once. It also leaked oil, was constantly getting itself jammed and gave people electric shocks.

Victory was built in Letchworth by the British Tabulating Machine Company under their chief engineer, Doc Keen. Once it was ready, there was a major problem of how to get it to Bletchley Park. The huge security it required would, the authorities thought, simply draw attention to it. In the end it was sent, quite openly, on the back of a lorry. It was installed in Hut 1 on 18 March 1940, just days before the invasion of Norway.

But the bombe would not solve the problem of the bigrams and trigrams. In 1937, the German navy had added their own complication to the Enigma machine. They chose a 'trigram' (three letters); from a code book known as the K Book and ciphered it to get the message setting. Then they turned the trigram into a 'bigram' (two letters) and sent it as a header to the message. It was this procedure which had foxed the Polish cryptographers before the war, and had eventually led them to approach the British and French. The K book had been captured early in 1940 but, without the annual bigram tables, it was hard to make any progress on naval Enigma at all.

**

Karl Dönitz had been a submarine commander, and a prisoner of war, during the First World War. He was austere, thin, supremely confident – so confident, in fact, that even Hitler dreaded his encounters with him. He also believed in the potential of submarine warfare against the shipping lanes if, as he feared, there was war again with the British.

He was in command of the German cruiser *Emden* – not the one which had sent the wrongly coded message picked up by Tranow, but a new version – and had gone on a long cruise in the summer of 1935, just as Mussolini was preparing to invade Abyssinia. He spent his times off duty working out the tactics for U-boats convinced that, if war came, the British would immediately adopt the convoy system which they had organised so successfully – but so late – in 1917. One submarine might happen on a convoy and maybe sink a ship, maybe two if they were lucky, but then the encounter would be over. Submarines could keep up with convoys on the surface, but dived – as they would need to be after an attack – and the convoy would just sweep by, even at their slow average speed of 6-7 knots. What could be done?

It was during the *Emden*'s voyage that Dönitz worked out the basis of the wolf pack system. When a U-boat found a convoy, they would not attack immediately. They would shadow from behind while they sent out signals about course and position until a pack of U-boats were in position, then they would take command of the attack from a position of more strength. It was a version of the system he had originally proposed in 1917, but the advent of short wave radios at sea made a difference. Sophisticated signals made the wolf packs possible. So when Dönitz was appointed to command the Kriegsmarine's U-boat fleet on his return that Autumn, he was determined to work out the system in the finest detail and to practice it until it was perfect.

Two technological elements were going to be crucial. A new kind of communications U-boat was designed, the Type IXB, with extra radio equipment. It required a wider range, and U-boats were now being built that had a radius of up to 10,000 miles without refuelling. It meant that coded signals were going to be absolutely vital. But it also meant, even if the codes remains secure, the enemy could still track position just by the direction the radio signals were coming from. Dönitz enforced a strict rule of radio silence, except when messages were urgent – weather reports, mine reports or convoy sightings. That meant that all signals need to be brief. As soon as war was declared, the U-boat service began work on a short code book so that signals could be compressed.

Dönitz kept up the pressure relentlessly for more submarines. The 1935 London Treaty had stipulated that the German navy would only ever be allowed to grow to be 35 per cent of the Royal Navy. By 1937, Dönitz had persuaded Grand Admiral Erich Raeder and Nazi high command that they would interpret the agreement to mean that submarines could go up to 100 per cent of the Royal Navy. By the autumn of 1939, the German navy had two modern battlecruisers, three 'pocket battleships', five cruisers and 17 destroyers. There were also 56 U-boats. Raeder told Hitler that all the navy could do was to show the world how to die with dignity.

**

In September 1939, the British remained ignorant about the vulnerability of their codes. Even so, some far-sighted naval signals experts were uneasy. After a spell as a signals specialist in Fisher's Mediterranean Fleet, Lord Louis Mountbatten tried to persuade the Admiralty to test out the more sophisticated American Telex-style coding machines on board ships, which the RAF was also doing. The navy had bought five of them, but the officers complained that they were too heavy and not useful at sea, and they were never adopted.

Mountbatten and his allies were also aware of the huge disadvantage the Royal Navy faced when it came to codes. The German navy could change their codes and settings once a month relatively simply. If the British wanted to do so, they would print their new code books in secure conditions as usual at the Oxford University Press, and then each one would require a personal courier to make sure it stayed safe, and to go within days all over the world, to the far-flung ships and shore establishments from Hong Kong to Iceland. It was a huge undertaking and one of the reasons they were so conservative on the subject of codes.

But the British were also over-confident about their ability to tackle the U-boats. They believed their Asdic invention, an early form of Sonar or underwater radar, was a killer technology which would effectively render the U-boats visible. When the first convoy sailed on 7 September, it was the prospect of encountering German surface raiders – a pocket battleship or a new battlecruiser – that really worried them. On the second day of the war, they put into effect long-standing plans for an air attack on the naval base of Wilhelmshaven, but the weather was overcast and the bombers only did minor damage. The real threat from German submarines was made doubly clear at the end of the second week of the war, when U29 sank the aircraft carrier *Courageous* which was being used most unwisely on anti-submarine duty.

Once again, the Royal Navy's global ambition was a disadvantage. Every convoy had to be protected by the kind of firepower that could see off an attack by a powerful surface unit. Every convoy needed destroyers or other escorts to be with them, at least half way across the Atlantic, whether or not they were going to be attacked. Since the Admiralty's trade division had assumed control of every British surface ship, and 2,400 could be expected to be at sea at any one time, they all had to be plotted and tracked. It was an enormous undertaking. They also had to position the fleet in such a way that they could prevent German raiders getting into the Atlantic, where they would be highly unlikely to be caught. The Icelandic sea lanes had to be patrolled night and day. Most important, all the potential intelligence – all the information from signals positioning, reconnaissance to code-breaking successes – had to be brought together so that it could be used effectively. The epicentre of this enormous operation was the Admiralty's OIC, their Operational Intelligence Centre, which held the reins between Bletchley Park and the navy, with underground bunkers in the Admiralty's ugly concrete 'Citadel' next to St James' Park, and with links to the Western Approaches command centre in Liverpool, which controlled the convoy traffic.

At their disposal, as well as Turing, Knox and their colleagues at Bletchley, were Coastal Command, but their planes had a short radius and no equipment for detecting U-boats. There was the navy's own reconnaissance versions of the Spitfire, their listening stations around the world and the direction finding equipment used to pinpoint enemy signals, carried on many destroyers at sea, and the lonely cruiser patrols in the far north around Iceland and the North Sea. There were not even enough ships, but there were certainly not enough planes. The enemy's signals traffic could be tracked, but it could very rarely be read.

A few days after the outbreak of war, the Admiralty recruited Paymaster Commander A. D. Wilson to run Naval Intelligence Department (NID) 10 to look at their own signals traffic to see what could be deduced from it, without being able to read it. Wilson was a biologist and an expert on the Great Barrier Reef, and he in turn recruited the keeper of the India section of the Victoria and Albert Museum. The answer was that a great deal of information was already available to the enemy, even without being able to read the signals – which, of course, they could. Wilson was able to deduce, for example, which British ships had been dispatched to hunt for the pocket battleship *Graf Spee* in the south Atlantic in December 1939.

It was a nervous moment. Unaware that the enemy was tracking convoy movements by reading signals, though not always fast enough to intercept them, and unable to read the signals themselves, the British did still have one option. The ships weren't available in sufficient numbers. The only alternative was to track the sources of U-boat signals and to help the convoys evade them.

This task fell to two of the most successful intelligence officers of the war, operating amidst great rivalry but great informality, next door to each other in Rooms 8 and 12 at the Admiralty's Citadel (NID 8). Both used huge tables covered with notes, sightings and conjectures, one to track the U-boats and the other to track the convoys and to propose evasions. The Submarine Tracking Room was established by Paymaster Commander Ernest Thring, who had done the same job in the First World War. He soon handed it over to Captain Rodger Winn. Winn was a former barrister who had offered his forensic skills to the navy for questioning prisoners (NID 1). For eleven hours every day, he stared at the table, trying to get into the head of Dönitz .

His opposite number in the Trade Plotting Room was Commander Richard Hall, who had naval intelligence in his genes – he was the son of Admiral Sir Reginald 'Blinker' Hall, the legendary head of naval intelligence during the First World War. Winn and Hall had a mildly bickering relationship but got on well. They shared a car to the Admiralty at seven every morning, and through the day would pit their wits against Dönitz's commanders and send their recommendations to Admiral Sir Percy Noble, commanding the Western Approaches from another tracking room in Liverpool, who would make the signals to the escorts.

As we know now, these were then decoded by Bonatz, Tranow and their teams at B-Dienst, often too late to pass onto the U-boats at sea but with enough time to pinpoint the convoys and the routes as they set sail from Liverpool or Halifax, Nova Scotia. The U-boats themselves were urged to keep radio silence to avoid the chance that their signals would be picked up and pinpointed in mid-Atlantic. The icy, damp and dangerous work of the escort and U-boat commanders was the war at the sharp end, but behind them on both sides were these dedicated logicians, painstakingly using what slithers of evidence they had, to get some narrow advantage in the war of nerves in the Atlantic.

**

As expected, it was the surface raiders which caused the navy most difficulty in the early months of the war. The pocket battleship *Graf Spee* scuttled itself in Montevideo just before Christmas 1939 but, through the early months of 1940, there were tragic encounters between heavy units of the Kriegsmarine and lightly armed merchant ships under navy command which were co-ordinating the convoys. Even by the Autumn of that year, the pocket battleship *Admiral Scheer* and the heavy cruiser *Admiral Hipper* were able to make sorties into the Atlantic, using decrypted signals to intercept convoy HX84 off Newfoundland, where they sank the armed merchant cruiser *Jervis Bay* and five merchant ships. *Admiral Hipper* also used decrypts to track the troop convoy WS5A on its way to the Middle East.

When the German trackers realised that the British were being forced to send their precious battleships to guard the convoys, it told them two things. First, that their surface raider strategy was working. It was forcing the British to spread their meagre resources too thinly. But second, it also reassured them that their naval Enigma codes were still impregnable. If the British were sending battleships with convoys, rather than keeping them in reserve to intercept a surface raider, then it meant they could not possibly be reading the signals. Enigma was safe.

A battleship looming out of the Atlantic mist was certainly an effective protection against surface raiders, but there was also a clue for the British naval intelligence if they had realised it. Why were the surface raiders able to roam the whole Atlantic and so often stumble upon the convoys? Why were the U-boats able to intercept convoys so regularly when they were keeping radio silence? The answer was that their signals and routes were being read by the other side. The Admiralty asked themselves the question but dismissed the idea that their own codes had been compromised on the grounds that these setbacks represented a run of bad luck. This was precisely what the German high command told themselves later in the war when Enigma signals were being regularly read.

The British remained confident that, because they had changed the basic five-digit cipher in August 1939, they were safe. In fact, it had taken Tranow only six weeks to use his knowledge to be able to read signals again. By the time of the Norwegian campaign, nearly half of all British naval signals were being read in full by B-Dienst. They changed the operational code after the fall of France a year later, but again

Tranow's team mastered the new basis by early the following year.

It was this knowledge that they used to good effect during the Norwegian campaign in April 1940, aware of exactly where the Home Fleet was and prepared to use their knowledge to jump on stragglers. This was how the aircraft carrier *Glorious* was attacked and sunk by *Scharnhorst* and *Gneisenau* off the coast of Norway. Meanwhile, Enigma continued to be just that. Even at Bletchley, there was some scepticism about whether a code system like Enigma could be cracked. Even Denniston, in charge at Bletchley Park, shared the Admiralty's doubts. "You know, the Germans don't intend you to read their stuff," he was heard to say before the war, "and I don't suppose you ever will."

**

It is possible to argue that the real deciding factor in the intelligence war lay elsewhere. The British approach to the problem to cryptography was completely different, even to the American approach. When Turing went to the USA to liaise with his American counterparts, he found they had mainly recruited lawyers. For some reason, so many of the British had gone out of their way to recruit oddballs, misfits and people with unusual interests. Hall in the Trade Tracking Room had tried to recruit "unorthodox people". The OIC at the Admiralty, and those who staffed the Citadel – what Churchill called "that vast monstrosity that weighs upon the Horse Guards Parade" – were unusual mavericks from a whole variety of different callings in civilian life. The same was even more true of Bletchley Park. The leading German code breakers like Tranow were professionals, steeped in their subject.

The British backed the gifted amateurs; the Germans the specialists and both approaches had something to be said for them. The real issue was how this expertise could be brought together. Even inside Bletchley, there were disputes between Knox and Denniston about who should be privy to the whole picture. In practice, the complete scene came together in the Citadel in the two tracking rooms, where Thring and Hall – and then Winn and Hall – brought the total information together and made judgements on the basis of the evidence.

This was not an approach favoured by the Nazis, whose deep suspicion of enemies within led them to divide the information so that nobody possessed the complete picture. It was separation, and suspicion, which put the German side at a disadvantage. But for the time being, the strategic advantage in the Atlantic lay with Dönitz.

3

Harry Hinsley, later Professor Sir Harry Hinsley and vice-chancellor of Cambridge University, was at the outbreak of war a slightly ramshackle young analyst in Hut 4 at Bletchley Park. He was only 20 and he was one of the most informal members of what was already one of the most informal wartime units. At one stage, in the first few months of the war, his colleagues in the hut clubbed together to buy him a new pair of corduroy trousers.

Hinsley had been studying medieval history in Cambridge and was now in charge of traffic analysis. His task was not so much to decode the messages but to notice patterns from where they were emerging from, and to draw conclusions. His breakthrough came early in April 1940 when he noticed a sudden increase in signal traffic in the Baltic area. Something was going on. On 7 April, he reported it to OIC at the Admiralty. They dismissed it. It was clear soon afterwards that something had indeed been happening. It was the German invasion of Norway.

Some weeks later, he began to notice something else. German naval signals using the Baltic frequencies were being repeated on other frequencies. After some days pondering what this meant, he began to suspect that the navy was about to move its surface ships from the Baltic to the Skagerrak, to intervene in the last stages of the Norwegian withdrawal. By the beginning of June, he was certain and was reporting to Rear-Admiral Norman Denning, head of OIC and the brother of Lord Denning, later Master of the Rolls, that the German navy was preparing for action in the North Sea.

What Hinsley did not know at the time was that British forces were at that very moment preparing for the humiliating evacuation from Norway. Nor was his information given the priority it deserved. In particular, it was not passed on to the captain of the carrier *Glorious,* sunk as we have seen by *Scharnhorst* and *Gneisenau.*

The trouble was that Hinsley's appearance and long hair did not endear him to the Admiralty, in the months before OIC and the staff in the Citadel came to appreciate the role of Station X at Bletchley Park. "That they should be jealous of his success is understandable," wrote Frank Birch, head of Bletchley's German navy section, in October. "That they should dislike him personally is a small matter, but that they should be obstructive is ruinous."

One of the outcomes of the disastrous Norwegian campaign was, after all, a change of government in the UK. It also brought about a reassessment of how the various elements of naval intelligence worked together, and it was not long before OIC began to rethink what they thought of Hinsley. There was also a rethink going on at U-boat headquarters at the same time.

**

In one of the most daring submarine attacks of the war, the U-boat commander Gunther Prien took U47 though the uncompleted defences of the Royal Navy's anchorage at Scapa Flow and sank the old battleship *Royal Oak*. It capsized and sank within minutes. Over 800 were drowned. He may also have damaged the retired battleship *Iron Duke*. The sinking of *Royal Oak* and *Courageous,* in consecutive months, began to make clear to the Admiralty what a menace the enemy submarines would be.

But they were not aware of a major problem that the U-boat commanders were facing. There was something wrong with their torpedoes. In the first few months of the war, U-boats had attacked the battleships *Nelson* and *Rodney*, believing that Winston Churchill – then the political head of the navy – was on board *Nelson*. They also attacked and hit the battlecruiser *Hood*. None of the torpedoes exploded. In April 1940, during the flurries of action off the coast of Norway, there were U-boat attacks on the cruisers *Cumberland* and *York*. Dönitz was sceptical – submarine commanders, like pilots, often believe they made hits when actually nothing of the kind happened. It was only when someone with the reputation of Prien complained – and he was a fierce disciplinarian – that Dönitz had to take notice.

Prien attacked and hit the battleship *Warspite*, but again the torpedo never went off. Dönitz began to suspect that his torpedoes were set to explode on the wrong magnetic settings and he ordered his U-boats out of Scandinavian waters until they could resolve the problem.

But out in the Atlantic, against merchant shipping, the U-boats were proving themselves again and again. Ever since B-Dienst had begun decoding convoy movement signals on 11 September 1939, the British had been at a serious disadvantage fighting the U-boat predators. The success of the Nazi Blitzkrieg in Western Europe had also handed Dönitz another major advantage. While the surface raiders could now operate out of Norway, from July 1940 his submarines could use bases directly on the Atlantic coast in France. He moved his U-boats to Lorient in Brittany, which would cut at least 450 miles from the outward journey to the Atlantic. He himself moved into the Chateau les Pignerolles as the flag officer of U-boats West (FdU West). Like Bletchley Park, FdU West had its own electricity generator.

At the same time, the British needed as many destroyers as possible in home waters to guard against the expected invasion. They simply could not be spared to protect convoys in the numbers that were needed. Dönitz had been freed from the need to support Norwegian operations by the withdrawal of allied troops, and he could concentrate entirely on the convoys. In July, U-boats sank 38 merchant ships. In September, it was 59 ships. In October it was 63. Imports to the UK had dropped by a quarter by October, to 45 million tons a year.

At that time, Dönitz still only had around seven seagoing U-boats available at any one time. But ten more were being completed every month and soon there would be enough of them at sea to be able to put his wolf pack tactics into operation. As he knew very well himself, this required beacon signals by the U-boat which first began shadowing the convoy. A huge radio mast at Angers would co-ordinate the U-boats at sea. Progress of the convoys would then by broadcast to the U-boat commanders. It was when they responded that there would be an opportunity to track the signal. Then the British could potentially pinpoint their positions in mid-Atlantic, to be plotted by Thring and his colleagues in the OIC submarine tracking room.

**

The shipping losses mounted. By the end of January 1941, with the terrible gales that hit the Atlantic that winter, Dönitz was again reduced in the number of sea-going U-boats he had available. But this time it was still as many as 22. He was also operating under another awkward setback. Tranow and his cryptographers at B-Dienst had been temporarily stymied by a change in Royal Navy cipher procedure, which meant they were unable to read the signals. Instead Dönitz began to send long-range bombers, which could take off from Bordeaux or Brest and fly to Norway to refuel and then return, to provide reconnaissance information about the convoys and their positions. He could then report them to the remaining U-boats on station.

In the event, it took only five months for Tranow and his team at B-Dienst to get back on top of British signals after the code – which they knew as 'Munich' (the cipher was codenamed 'Cologne') – was changed in August 1940. By February, Churchill came to believe that the nation could face starvation within four months if the Atlantic losses continued to rise. The House of Commons went into secret session that month so that he could set out his plans, coining a phrase which has come to define the longest battle of the war, the Battle of the Atlantic. "The only thing that ever really frightened me during the war was the U-boat peril," he wrote later.

A Battle of the Atlantic cabinet committee would meet weekly, chaired by the First Sea Lord, Sir Dudley Pound. In the meantime, two immediate measures were coming to fruition. The Lend-Lease Act was signed into law in the USA on 11 March, whereby the USA would swap 50 old American destroyers to boost the terrible shortage of convoy escorts, in return for long leases on British naval bases around the world. There was also an agreement that, short of declaring war or doing anything that might bring about war or undermine their neutrality, the US navy would take over the duties of escorting convoys operating out of Greenland, Newfoundland and the West Indies, and of course along the American coast. It was a policy that would lead to fatal clashes between U-boats and American destroyers, culminating in the sinking of the *Reuben James*, and Woody Guthrie's famous rallying song that is still sung to this day.

There was also to be a change of tactics among the convoy escorts, once they had been reinforced by the ancient four-funnelled American destroyers. If they encountered a U-boat, they would not just rush back to protect the ships in the convoy after an attack, which meant they often simply allowed attacking U-boats to lie low and get away unscathed. They would carry on the chase until they had caught them or lost them completely.

Hinsley's traffic analysis was now being taken seriously in OIC. He was known as the Cardinal and congratulated everywhere he went, at least by the few insiders who knew what he was achieving. His visits to the Citadel were celebrated and inspiring. But what Knox, Turing and their colleagues really needed was a break: in particular, they needed the K Book and the bigram tables. And that break might just have to come from the high seas.

**

In the early hours of the morning on 12 February 1940, the British minesweeper *Gleaner* detected an underwater noise. They dropped depth charges on what they believed must be a U-boat, and the explosions were so powerful that the lights on board *Gleaner* were knocked out. The sea around was quiet, when suddenly out of the depths of the Clyde estuary emerged the conning tower of what turned out to be U33.

On the bridge of the *Gleaner*, Lieutenant Commander Hugh Price realised there was an opportunity for capture and rapidly came alongside. The crew of the submarine were soon on deck, shouting wildly, when a huge explosion tore the conning tower apart, damaging the minesweeper's engines. The remains of U33 drifted out of reach and sank. Local trawlers rushed to the scene, but only 17 of the crew of 42 were rescued. They did not include the commanding officer, Commander Hans-Wilhelm von Dresky, who had already won himself a reputation as a humanitarian, towing the lifeboats of those he had sunk, even firing his own distress rockets to attract attention from potential rescuers.

But the real surprise came when the survivors were searched. They found a number of peculiar Bakelite wheels in their pockets, which – in their hurry to escape – they had forgotten to drop in the sea. They turned out to be rotor wheels from an Enigma machine. These were important, especially when – during April – the German naval trawler *Polares* was seized by the destroyer *Griffin,* and enough material seized to begin to reconstruct the bigram tables. Bletchley would need one day's signals with at least 200 of them to have the built up a selection with enough alignments which were not down to chance. The first day where naval signals could be interpreted was 8 May 1940, though it took until November to read any of them.

But these captures did remind the British, wrestling with Enigma, that there was an obvious way out of their difficulties. They might find cribs which could be fed into the *bombe* computers, and one of these might unlock the Enigma settings for the month – if they could find the bigram tables – but the whole process could be short-circuited by capturing a machine, preferably with the correct settings set up and the codes for the month.

It was a difficult and frustrating period at Bletchley Park. Those concerned with air force or army settings for Enigma were kept busy by simple decoding, but the navy cryptographers were still largely in the dark. Some people almost preferred it that way: Turing said later that he chose the naval signals conundrum because "I could have it to myself".

Actually, of course, he could have no such thing: too much depended on it. "Turing and Twinn are brilliant," wrote Frank Birch in Hut 4, speaking also of Peter Twinn, the mathematician who would take over from Knox when he became ill in 1942. "But like many brilliant people, they are not practical. They are untidy, they lose things, and they can't copy right."

Knox complained about Turing. "I have just, but only just, enough authority and ability to keep his ideas in some sort of order and discipline," he said. "But he is very nice about it all." Worse, he said, the bombe machines were virtually monopolised by air force intelligence, Turing was working in what he believed was an 'unsystematic' way, and Hinsley's cribs – his clues about the meanings of some of the phrases – were "not certain at all".

"The long and the short of it," wrote Birch as 1940 wore on, "is that the Navy is not getting its fair does." Birch himself was urging a scheme to send out random messages on the same frequency, in the hope that they might attract a standard reply which might be used as a crib. But the main chance still seemed to be the most likely possibility. So on 29 August 1940, the Admiralty send this letter to all the commanding officers in home ports:

> "It is known that many German Navel Signals are ciphered on a machine, a photograph of a ciphering machine is reproduce, any machine of this type is discovered on a German man-of war should be carefully packed and forwarded to the Director of Naval Intelligence, Admiralty, in charge of an officer by the quickest possible route."

While they waited for the breakthrough, the Bletchley code breakers were making progress with the Italian naval code, especially since July 1940, when Mussolini entered the war on Hitler's side.

**

"These have knelled your fall and ruin, but your ears were far away/English lassies rustling papers through the sodden Bletchley day." The lines were written by Dilly Knox about Mussolini after the crushing defeat of an Italian naval squadron at the Battle of Matapan. His poem stayed classified as secret until 1978.

Because, while struggling with German naval Enigma was proving frustrating, Italian naval Enigma – with no bigrams and trigrams – was altogether easier. The breakthrough for reading Italian naval Enigma came from Mavis Lever, one of Knox's assistants at Bletchley Park, later the garden writer Mavis Batey. It was she who noticed the clue. It was an Italian signal and she realised, reading through it, that the letter L didn't appear at all. One of the few weaknesses of the Enigma system was that a letter would never appear as itself. It was odd, therefore, that it was never used. She guessed that this particular message might just be a dummy just using the letter L.

The ability to read Italian naval signals led to what was the major victory over the Italian fleet at Cape Matapan in March 1941, which led to the destruction of five Italian warships. It was based on partial intelligence based on reading a decoded signal about an Italian naval exercise.

The Mediterranean Fleet commander-in-chief, Sir Andrew Cunningham, had served with Fisher in the 1930s. He found it hard to believe that this mere slither of intelligence would result in any kind of action, but he set off for the golf club outside Alexandria, speaking loudly about his weekend of relaxation, aware that the Japanese ambassador was listening. The fleet had already sailed, but it must have seemed inconceivable that a serious action was intended without the admiral. Yet, by the evening, and unnoticed, he was aboard his flagship *Warspite*, steaming north.

The news that the Italian battle fleet had been sighted came when he was in the bath. The Battle of Matapan that followed was one of the most decisive naval engagements of the war. Afterwards, Knox was called by the Director of Naval Intelligence, Rear-Admiral John Godfrey, and was told they had won a great victory in the Mediterranean and it was "entirely due to him and his girls". Cunningham visited Bletchley himself to thank them personally, and Mavis Lever and her friends played a practical joke on him, backing him onto a newly whitewashed wall in his pristine navy blue admiral's uniform. It was that kind of place.

4

Godfrey was the spider at the heart of OIC. He was Director of Naval Intelligence and was in direct charge of Naval Intelligence Division (NID) 17 and had been since January 1939, when he was plucked from his position as commanding officer of the battlecruiser *Repulse*. There he had met and impressed the new First Sea Lord – Dudley Pound, the operational head of the Royal Navy – because he was so widely read.

Godfrey was known as meticulous and demanding. It was his job to co-ordinate naval intelligence across the divisions and, under his leadership, NID 17 rapidly grew to 2,000 strong, dealing with signals, coded and decoded, arriving every day by courier in especially sealed boxes – and these were signals from both sides: Godfrey understood, in a way that his German opposite numbers failed to in quite the same way, that naval intelligence also required a complete knowledge about what your own side was doing. Until the advent of the Special Operations Executive, it was Godfrey's job to launch secret operations – from Sefton Delmer's fake radio stations to Hinsley's fake messages, and a great deal in between. It was also his task to liaise between naval intelligence and the sea lords who ran the navy, and who operated out of the other doors along the corridor at the Admiralty Building in Whitehall.

Godfrey was sceptical about cryptography, believing that Knox's code breakthrough in 1916 had bred the kind of over-confidence which had undermined the other branches of naval intelligence in the inter-war years. But he also did Bletchley Park a favour by coming up with his own colour code system that gave a proper respect for their ability to read signals. He quickly became fed up with explaining how reliable his intelligence was. As a result, he invented the grading system that both hid the fact intelligence came from reading signals, but also managed to give the information gleaned the respect it deserved.

Godrey's office was Room 40, the famous office which had belonged to Admiral 'Blinker' Hall in the First World War. He was supposed to sleep under concrete in the Citadel at nights but very quickly found this did not lead to restful snoozing and moved into Hall's old flat at 36 Curzon Street.

Room 40 was at the end of the main corridor at the Admiralty, by tall windows looking out to the west, across the garden of 10 Downing Street over St James' Park and Horse Guards Parade. To get there, you needed to go through Room 39, where Godfrey's assistants worked, in the frenetic atmosphere that was described as like a newspaper newsroom. Like Bletchley, it was filled with informal mavericks; unlike Bletchley, these were often mavericks with overweening self-confidence – the kind of people who could face down a stare from the First Sea Lord and survive. It was known by insiders as 'the zoo'.

In the prime position in Room 39, right by the door to Godfrey's office, was the desk belonging to his assistant, Ian

Fleming, a man known to history as the creator of James Bond. Fleming shared all the most obvious characteristics of the zoo. He was informal, creative and hugely self-confident, a "giant among name-droppers" when it came to getting things done.

Fleming had also been wrestling with the problem of Enigma and the need for more information about the code books. He was, even then, a master plotter. After the capture of the Enigma rings from U33 in February 1940, Fleming began to develop a bold plan. So bold that it was hard to see how it might be achieved, but Fleming kept pushing.

The idea was that they would borrow a German plane and ditch the pilot into the sea, where he would be picked up by a naval rescue boat. The fake pilot would then take control of the boat, kill the crew and sail to the UK together with the boat's Enigma machine and codebooks. It was known, perhaps not surprisingly, as Operation Ruthless.

By the autumn 1940, the plan had come up against an unresolveable problem. There was no German plane available and it was 'postponed indefinitely'. The team at Bletchley Park was bitterly disappointed. "Turing and Twinn came to me like undertakers cheated of a fresh corpse two days ago," wrote Frank Birch, "all in a stew about the cancellation of Operation Ruthless."

The operation had been cancelled, but the problem remained. How could the code-breakers get hold of a machine and the various tables and codebooks they would need to read the signals, and to reconstruct the wiring of the machine and the rotors? The months went by and the merchant shipping losses continued to rise. Churchill coined the phrase about the 'Battle of the Atlantic'. The crisis was developing. Something had to be done.

**

In the late 1930s, most naval nations were developing a new kind of ship, which was usually known as a 'super-destroyer'. They would be faster, better armed and more effective than the previous models and, in the UK, they were known as the Tribal class. They were rakish, streamlined and powerful and 16 of them had been launched before the outbreak of war. They were due to be at the epicentre of all the naval actions in the first half of the war, and to bear the brunt of the losses – no less than 12 had been sunk by 1945.

The Tribals made up two flotillas of destroyers at the outbreak of war, and they were elite commands: Philip Vian in *Cossack* led the 4th Destroyer Flotilla, and had hit the headlines in 1940 when he captured the supply ship *Altmark* and released the merchant navy prisoners on board. Gresham Nicholson in *Somali* led the 6th Destroyer flotilla, with their distinctive single white stripe on the second funnel. Nicholson had recently handed over his command to Captain Clifford Caslon and, under Caslon, *Somali* was about to play a key role in the next chapter of the battle against Enigma at sea. Caslon provided the command post for the commando raid on the Lofoten Islands.

As *Somali* swept in at dawn on 4 March 1941, they passed the German naval trawler *Krebs*. There was no time to deal with it, if there was to be an element of surprise, but *Krebs* fired bravely at the destroyer, hitting the flags above the bridge.

Somali's 4.7 inch guns were brought to bear, and a few moments later, *Krebs* was a smoking wreck, steaming slowly in a circle.

A few hours later, after a successful raid which destroyed the German fish oil facilities, Caslon sent one of his lieutenants to search the wreck and help the wounded. Lieutenant Sir Marshall Warmington went across with a landing party of three, all armed with pistols. When they arrived, the five surviving crew of *Krebs* were on the deck waving a white flag. Warmington knew nothing about Enigma, but headed off to find the captain's cabin. One of the drawers was locked and, after a fruitless tussle with the lock, he shot it off with his pistol. The bullet ricocheted worryingly around the room. Inside were two mysterious discs, which he failed to recognise, but which turned out to be rotors for an Enigma machine.

Three quarters of an hour later, Caslon was getting impatient. Standing off the smoking wreck of Krebs made them vulnerable to submarine attack, and he signalled that the boarding party should return to the ship. As he left the cabin, Warmington grabbed a set of papers entitled *Sclüsseltafeln M-Allgemein 'Heimische Gewässer' Kennwort HAU. Prufnummer 1566.* Then he headed back to *Somali,* unaware that he had unwittingly made an important discovery.

The papers reached Hut 8 at Bletchley Park on 12 March, and turned out to be exactly what Turing and Twinn had needed – the Enigma settings for home waters. Unfortunately, they were the settings for February, which meant they were already out of date. But they had the February messages available in the original coded form and were attempting to decode messages sent on February 27 on the day the gift from *Somali* arrived. Having the settings allowed them to reconstruct part of the bigram tables and that meant that Turing's Banburismus procedure could be tried again.

Even here, there were difficulties. They were moving achingly slowly. Many of the messages for March seemed to be dummies, which messed up the statistics – one of the most important tools in a cryptographer's toolbox is knowing the exact proportion of each letter used in the original language, and it allowed them to tell when there were these all-important overlaps of different settings. By early May, only eight days of messages in April had been painstakingly read. And if decoding could only go at that speed, it was difficult to know which signals to prioritise.

To make matters worse, Dönitz was getting suspicious. The successful record built up by OIC at pinpointing U-boats in the Atlantic and re-routing convoys to avoid them was worrying him and he confided in his diary in April that he was afraid someone was revealing where the submarines were. As a result, U-boats were given special keys which could keep their messages secret from other parts of the naval Enigma network.

Bletchley was not represented at Churchill's Battle of the Atlantic committee in Whitehall, though Rear-Admirals Clayton and Denning were there from OIC. They had to report that the sinkings were creeping up again after the lull during the poor weather of the end of 1940. There were 21 merchant vessels sunk in January 1941, 58 in February and there were only 12 definite sinkings of Dönitz's big ocean-going U-boats in the whole of the previous year. April brought one of the biggest convoy disasters so far. Convoy SC26, from Sydney in Nova Scotia, was attacked by a wolf pack of eight U-boats and as many as 11 ships had been sunk. But it was just this moment of fear and frustration that led the way to a breakthrough on naval Enigma.

**

It had been known that weather forecasting was a major problem for the German war effort. They no longer had access to the kind of weather data that was available to the British simply because they were further to the west. It made it difficult to make sure than bombing raids or other major military operations were planned with the changing weather in mind. This was especially so in the run up to Operation Sealion, the Nazi plan for the invasion of Britain. It was absolutely essential that they had accurate weather forecasts if that was ever going to take place. As the D-Day planners knew all too well four years later, bad weather could sink an invasion in more ways than one.

So to provide themselves with the kind of weather forecasts, and weather data on which they were based, the Germans had for some time been sending small lightly armed trawlers, manned mainly by civilians, into the far north of the North Sea, to watch over the emerging weather systems in the Atlantic and Arctic. Nobody paid them much attention.

But thanks to the unexpected discovery of an Enigma code book in *Krebs*, a naval trawler, it did concentrate the minds of those who were wrestling with codes at sea. It was also clear that some of those messages being decoded so laboriously were weather reports. If they were sending messages from off Iceland in code then they must have Enigma machines and codebooks on board the weather ships. The proposal to seize one came from Harry Hinsley. The captured crew might throw the machine and the May code settings overboard, but equally they might – if the deed was done fast enough – leave the June settings in the safe.

Once again, the task was given to Caslon on *Somali*. The key was to avoid suspicion, either beforehand to give the weather ship warning, but afterwards too. They had to give the impression that the ship was seized accidentally. If it seemed at all possible that they were actually after Enigma, then there would never be a chance to repeat the exercise, and the settings would be changed. So *Somali* was embedded in a fleet of the cruisers *Birmingham, Edinburgh* and *Manchester* and four destroyers, which was ordered to rendezvous north of the Faroe Islands on 6 May, and which then steamed back towards Scotland for three hours, before returning very early the next morning. It was to look like an exercise.

Finally, at 5pm on 7 May, *Somali* sighted smoke on the horizon. It was the German weather ship *München*. Caslon laid a smokescreen and swept in at 32 knots, opening fire from three miles away. It was vital that the crew should panic and forget the codebooks. Coming alongside, Warmington leapt aboard and caught the radio operator sending a desperate distress message. It was clear that the Enigma machine had already gone over the side.

Caslon asked for an urgent prize crew from the cruiser *Edinburgh,* and it included Captain Jasper Haines from OIC. He went straight down into *München*'s captain's cabin and returned with a sack filled with papers. *München*'s crew were captured unscathed, except for a bullet hole in the foot. Haines and the sack were despatched to Scapa Flow by the destroyer *Nestor.* The Admiralty put out a statement saying that *München* had been scuttled by her crew, in an attempt to allay German fears about the security of Enigma. But three days later, the sack was with Turing and Twinn and the papers included the elusive settings for June.

More than anything else, the weather ship had provided a means by which naval Enigma could be read on a more routine basis. It was up to OIC now to reap the benefits.

5

The *enfant terrible* of the U-boat service was Lieutenant-Commander Fritz-Julius Lemp. He had born in China in 1913, in Tsingtao, the Imperial German navy's far eastern base. He was disobedient, witty and difficult and he was loved by his crews. The day war broke out, he was in command of U30 and west of Ireland, which – in flagrant defiance of Dönitz 's regulations about identifying features on conning towers – carried a logo of his dog Schnurzl painted by Georg Högel, a former art student, now his radio operator. That same day, 3 September 1939, Lemp sighted what turned out to be the Cunard liner *Athenia*. Believing this was an armed merchant cruiser, a warship, he fired two torpedoes without warning. *Athenia* sank with the deaths of 117 passengers and crew.

The Americans were particularly horrified because of the loss of life, but the British were also surprised. It marked the end of the brief life of the submarine treaty agreement which stipulated that passenger ships would not be sunk by either side without warning. In Berlin, Goebbels had announced that the loss of the *Athenia* had been sabotage by the British to undermine relations with the USA.

When Lemp arrived home and admitted he had carried out the sinking after all, he was put under arrest and then released the following day. He was still one of Dönitz's most successful U-boat captains and it made no sense to keep him behind bars.

He spent the following months irritating his superiors, or any other disciplinarians he ran across. He allowed his men to party until the early hours. He played English dance music on board, despite a strict ban and he carried on a running battle with his first officer, who had been furious that Lemp had allowed a British survivor on board and offered him a cigarette. On one occasion, ordered to file weather reports and then go back to Lorient, Lemp lost his temper and sent a signal which just said "Shit".

The second half of 1940 was known as the 'happy time' among the U-boat crews. It was a period when the handful of crews and U-boats built formidable reputations for their bold ability to follow and destroy convoy shipping. People like Gunther Prien, Otto Kretschmer, Joachim Schepke and Lemp were heroes in the German navy. In November 1940, Lemp was given his reward. He was put in command of one of the new bigger submarines, U110, one of the Type 1XB designed with double the number of torpedoes, and – because of the experience of the danger of maritime aircraft – an AA gun as well as a 4.1 inch gun. U110 had been built in Bremen, was 251 feet long and had an operating radius of 8,700 miles without needing to refuel.

Setting sail from Kiel in March 1941 in the week of the Lofoten Raid, Lemp was ordered to take the construction worker Ulrich Kruze to see one of the submarines he had been building in action. Because of Kruze we have an account of one of U110's most traumatic voyages. Lemp sighted the convoy HX112 from Canada and four other U-boats rushed to the scene. The resulting melee in the following days saw the death of Schepke on U100, picked up by onboard radar by the destroyer *Vanoc*, the first time a U-boat had been sunk in this way. It also saw the sinking of U99 and the rescue of Kretschmer, later to become an admiral in the post-war West German navy.

Six weeks later, Lemp found himself 300 miles south west of Greenland, shadowing the 35 merchant ships comprising convoy OB318 from Liverpool, which had assembled off the coast of Scotland on 2 May. It was midday on 9 May, just two days since the capture of *München,* and Commander Joe Baker-Cresswell had recently assumed command of the convoy escort, on board the destroyer *Bulldog*. There was some confusion in Lorient about the situation, and they had believed at one stage they were dealing with two convoys.

The same convoy had also been shadowed by U94 which had already attacked and sunk two ships. U201 was also dashing as fast as possible on the surface to join in and had arrived that morning. Lemp would have preferred to wait until the new escort flotilla arrived from Iceland that evening for the last leg to Halifax. But he also knew that a bird in hand was often worth two in the bush. Also U201's commander Adalbert Schnee wanted to attack that morning. Lemp moved onto the right flank.

U-boat tactics had to take account of the speed of a submarine on the surface, which could keep up with convoys, and its speed when submerged. They could shadow from behind on the surface, but – when it came to getting into an attack position, which would require diving – they would have to edge out in front. So Baker-Cresswell's tactics were to spread the bulk of his escort out in front of the convoy to listen for submarines. It was an exhausting schedule with four hours on watch followed by eight hours off, scouring the implacable sea, through the radar and the old-fashioned way, with naval binoculars, designed to give the maximum magnification without tiring the eyes. It was still dull: British naval researchers found that officers on watch from a submarine conning tower would spend an average of 30 minutes in that four hours cleaning their lenses.

Bulldog was then ten years old, which was almost out-of-date with the speed of technological development. The two funnelled destroyer had been build in Wallsend in 1930, and its crew of 138 had been in the East Indies and the Mediterranean only the previous year. Destroyers had been in the front line of the naval war so far. Half of *Bulldog's* B class would not survive the war, three of them sinking within a few weeks of each other during the terrible summer of 1940. When she was built, she had been capable of 35 knots. Now she was having to zigzag day and night at the speed of only 8 knots, the slowest merchant ship in the convoy. And at that latitude, sixteen hours a day could be spent in darkness.

Baker-Cresswell was inevitably known by his crew after the phonetic alphabet 'Able Baker Cresswell'. He was no longer expecting U-boat attacks so far west, though five of his escorts were spread out ahead of the convoy as usual. Suddenly, there was a column of water that indicated an underwater explosion next to the merchant ship *Esmond*. The ship settled slowly into the water and disappeared. Just as Baker-Cresswell was signalling an order for an emergency turn to port to avoid torpedoes, there was another explosion beside the *Bengore Head*. It was then that one of the escorts, the corvette *Aubretia*, picked up a signal from a submerged submarine on the starboard side of the convoy and set off in pursuit. *Bulldog* raced to their assistance.

**

Lemp had fired four torpedoes in quick succession. There had been an audible explosion in the distance echoing through the icy sea, but there was also an immediate problem. The fourth torpedo had failed to leave the tube. Sea water had been pumped into the tube ready to fire, but it had failed to shoot out again with a burst of compressed air as it should have done. Consequently the submarine was now too heavy at the bows and Lemp began to lose control.

There was a short struggle to rebalance the trim and, when Lemp was finally satisfied and his crew breathed a sigh of relief, there was the warning throb of a warship coming straight towards them. Lemp ordered U110 to dive and they could hear the literally deafening roar of depth charges exploding all around them.

The experience of a depth charge attack has been described as a terrifying, disorientating ordeal. You could hear the steel plates of the submarine grinding together as the pressures mounted from the depths, together with the extraordinary pressure of an underwater explosion. There were ominous cracks and, as always on such occasions, it was never quite clear how far down they had gone – and what it would take to rise again.

Silence at last. They looked for reassurance from Lemp, who was leaning theatrically against a periscope. "It's OK," he said. "We're all going to be fine. You don't think I'm going to let them catch me and shoot me, do you?"

It was a reference to the *Athenia* sinking eighteen months before and it was the kind of robust humour that was called for at this nervous moment. Then the reports began coming into the control room. They weren't good. The rudders were damaged. The batteries were giving off poisonous chlorine fumes, which they did in contact with water. The wheel that was used to blow the ballast tanks had come off. The depth meters had failed. The engineer Hans-Joachim Eichelborn struggled quickly to fit new pressure gauges to the main cooling water pipes for the diesel engines, so he knew they were not actually sinking, but there was the noise of pressurised air escaping from somewhere. If they ever wanted to get to the surface, they would have to blow the tanks soon. The deciding factor was discovering that one of the propeller shafts had bent. It was clear they had no choice. They had to surface.

"We must wait and see what happens," said Lemp quietly. "I want you all now to think of home, or something beautiful."

It was a terrifying moment. The crew waited for the pressures on the hull to increase until it crushed them and the sea water rushed in as they sank to the depths of the Atlantic. Instead, there was a surprise. Suddenly, the boat was rocking. They must be on the surface after all. "Last stop!" shouted Lemp, like a bus conductor. "Everybody out!"

**

Bulldog could see U110 on the surface dead ahead and Baker-Cresswell ordered his engine room to increase speed to ram. As they got closer it was clear that the crew were on the deck and he put *Bulldog*'s engines into reverse to come alongside. Then there was a moment of indecision: were the crew actually clustering around the gun? *Bulldog* opened fire again with a machine gun until Baker-Cresswell confirmed that those aboard the U-boat were actually jumping into the water.

The scene on deck of U110 was almost as terrifying as it had been under water. Two warships were making fast towards them – the destroyers *Bulldog* and *Broadway* – and they were shooting. Shells and bullets were flying overhead. The journalist on board, Helmut Ecke, wrote later that he saw a man's head blown to pieces next to him. He leapt into the water forgetting that his lifejacket had not yet been inflated. Then came the crucial moment. The radio operator, Högel, climbed up the conning tower and asked Lemp if he should destroy the codebooks and Enigma machine. "The U-boat is sinking!" shouted Lemp. Högel went back inside to get the codebooks, but remembered his own notebooks and poetry for his girlfriend and got them instead.

By now, *Broadway* was also approaching fast, as Baker-Cresswell signalled desperately to them to keep clear, then used his loudhailer to shout: "do not ram!" Lieutenant Commander Thomas Taylor on *Broadway* had been trying to get alongside to put a depth charge under U110 to stop her diving again. But as his destroyer swept up, he caught the U110's fin and tore a hole in *Broadway's* hull.

Lemp and his first lieutenant, Dietrich Loewe, made sure than the vents had been opened and jumped into the sea themselves, the last to leave. It was only when they were half way between U110 and *Bulldog* that it became clear that something was not right. The submarine was not actually sinking after all, at least not nearly so fast. Lemp shouted that they should go back, but a wave swept Loewe away and instead he made for *Bulldog*.

What happened to Lemp has never been clear. The British side suggests that he was never seen again. The German side suggests that he was shot before he could reboard his submarine. There are no eye-witness accounts either way. Perhaps that is only to be expected, though – if he was shot – it could only have been from *Broadway* or *Bulldog*, and both were busy with other activities at the time.

On board *Bulldog*, the same thought which had run through Lemp's mind was also dawning on Baker-Cresswell – the U-boat next to him was not actually sinking. "By God!" he said on *Bulldog*'s bridge. "We'll do a Magdeburg!" *Magdeburg* had been a German cruiser, captured by the Russians in 1914 with codebooks intact.

As the prisoners were being taken below, he briefed his young sub-lieutenant, David Balme, who had been next to him on the bridge. He told him to get on board as quickly as he could and to look for any signal books. Balme was only twenty and he was the navigating officer and – because they were one officer short at the time – he had also been in charge of the guns as they dashed towards the stricken U-boat. He took an eight-man crew with him and rowed across what was a heaving, oily swell. As they approached the bobbing submarine, their whaler was picked up by a wave and hurled onto the deck, damaging it but wedging it below the conning tower. Gingerly, but as fast as they could, they extricated themselves and climbed to the top to find the hatch.

The hatch sprung back easily, revealing another hatch below. It was a nervous moment. Balme indicated that he would go down the ladder first. He was only too aware that there may be members of the crew waiting for him below, or booby traps set, and the submarine was also believed to be sinking. He found he couldn't easily climb down the ladder into the control room and hold his pistol at the same time. He put it back in its holster. "Going down those ladders and thinking there may be Germans ready to shoot you ... was terrifying," he told the BBC years later. "We couldn't believe that they would have just abandoned this submarine. It was something that haunted me for fifteen or twenty years afterwards."

In the control room, Balme got his revolver out again. He found that the watertight doors were open fore and aft. There was a large jagged splinter from the conning tower and there was the sound of air escaping from somewhere. All the lighting was on, giving a "strange ghostly effect". There was no smell of chlorine gas, so Balme and his team set their gasmasks aside. They also put down their revolvers, because they seemed more of a hazard than a safety precaution. They were alone.

On the deck above, Balme's team had managed to raise the retractable bollards and began the search for a towing wire.

Bulldog came alongside and dropped one off for them. Downstairs, everything was quiet except for the swaying in the swell – U110 was still leaning about 15 degrees to port. Balme shouted up for the team to join him, telling them to discard anything that was obviously a magazine or reading material but to grab anything else. None of them could read German and the papers seemed to have been strewn everywhere. He organised a human chain to pass things up to the control room when the telegraphist came out of the radio room. "There's something rather interesting I want to show you," he said. In the radio room, a tiny space, was a machine like a typewriter, screwed to the table. They could see that, when you pressed one key another one lighted up. Balme told him to unscrew it and send it up with the rest.

Sandwiches appeared after the first hour and a half, sent over from *Bulldog,* and a replacement boat sent over from *Broadway,* because the original one had now been completely smashed by the waves. Balme searched Lemp's cabin, sitting down at Lemp's own desk to eat his sandwiches and finding Lemp's iron cross. He found a secure locker, broke the lock but discovered that it only contained first aid equipment. With great effort, they disconnected the sound detection equipment but, to their disappointment, found that it was too big to get through the hatches. They also failed to turn off the submarine's engine.

Balme also found a cine-camera in the radio room and he took a series of pictures of the wireless equipment and any other sophisticated equipment he could find. He later found the range on the camera had been set for 25 feet so assumed they would not come out. He and his team also found plenty of tinned ham, corned beef, cigars and cigarettes, and a well stocked galley. There was even a plate of shrimps in the radio room.

But for all the excitement, it was a frightening time. Balme and his men spent five hours inside the swaying remains of U110, listening to the sound of depth charges going off in the distance, as the escorts chased U20, which had torpedoed and sunk the freighter *Gregalia* and hit *Empire Cloud*, which was then abandoned (it was salvaged later). At one stage, *Bulldog* was forced to leave them when a periscope was reported, setting them adrift in a sinking submarine in the middle of the north Atlantic. "This was indeed a desolate and awful moment," Balme wrote later. "There was I, with my boarding-party, aboard U110, in the middle of the Atlantic, alone with no ships in sight with the wind and sea gradually increasing.

By 4pm, they had done all they could, so they battened down the hatches, crossed their fingers and waited. An hour or so later, they were relieved to see *Bulldog* returning, and with more help from the Chief Bosun's mate, they managed to secure the tow line and finally, at 6.30pm – tired and pleased – they made their way back to the ship. It was at this point that the crucial Admiralty signal arrived. The significance of what had been happening had not been lost on them:

> "Your operation is to be referred to as Operation Primrose in all future signals. Reference to it is to be prefaced Top Secret and signals to be made only in cipher."

A second signal arrived shortly afterwards and was sent to all the ships which had been involved: "Operation Primrose to be treated with greatest secrecy and few people allowed to know as possible." It is ironic to think that these signals would have been read by B-Dienst, but their significance would not have been clear. It was very clear to OIC. The capture of a German U-boat might have propaganda value, but that publicity would be inconvenient if it meant that the enemy began to wonder if they had got their hands on the codebooks.

Even so, the submarine was considered worth saving. The Admiralty rushed to send a submarine expert out to see if U110 could be kept afloat by Sunderland flying boat, but it was clear by the morning that this would be too late. At 11am, it was horribly obvious to Baker-Cresswell and his crew that U110 could not survive. They cut the tow rope and the U-boat slipped below the waves for the last time. That evening another signal was received:

> "Primrose having sunk makes it no repeat no less
> important that the fact of having had her in our hands
> should remain secret. This fact is to be rigorously
> impressed on all who have any knowledge of the fact."

Balme settled down to write his report, and to puzzle over a handful of peculiarities that still bothered him. Why, for example, were both conning tower hatches closed if Lemp had believed U110 was doomed? Was it force of habit? Or something else?

Early on 11 March, *Bulldog* reached Hvalfjord in Iceland, and refuelled before setting off with the prisoners to Scapa Flow. Baker-Cresswell acted on the order and assembled the crew, explaining that the prisoners must not know that the capture had taken place – they had been below when the drama was unfolding and Balme was aboard, so they must not discover it now. His crew found a boat hook from U110 in full view on the deck and had to hide it.

Bulldog arrived in Scapa Flow on the evening of the following day and two officers from OIC came straight aboard and made for Baker-Cresswell's cabin. They were staggered to see how much paperwork had been rescued, and to see some of it hanging up to dry already. "Oh, surely not this!" one of them exclaimed. when he saw the machine. "We have waited the whole war for one of these." There was a long photography session, in case the originals were destroyed in an air raid. Baker-Cresswell was told not to worry about losing the U-boat. "From our point of view it was a good thing," the officer, Lieutenant Allon Bacon, told him. "We can now keep all this quiet."

Who could be told? Baker-Cresswell said he would have to tell the Commander-in-Chief, and Admiral Sir Percy Noble, in command of the Western Approaches. "Yes," said Bacon, "but no-one else."

Bacon was in London by 6pm the following day, 13 May. Three hours later, he was driving through the gates of Bletchley Park on his way to Hut 4 to see Harry Hinsley. The codebooks were rushed into action and from that day, German naval messages began to take as little as a week to decode. It would prove important in the following week.

In Scapa Flow, Baker-Cresswell went to see the Commander-in-Chief of the Home Fleet, Sir John Tovey, on board his flagship, the battleship *King George V.* "You fellows get all the fun," said Tovey. "I just stay here and wait for the German fleet to come out. It's a dull job." But the following week, it would not be dull at all.

6

On 20 May 1941, the neutral Swedish cruiser *Gotland* sighted the powerful German battleship *Bismarck* at sea and leaving the Baltic, presumably up the coast of Norway. They reported it to their own admiralty, and 'Major Törnberg' – not his real name, as it turned out, but a half-Norwegian diplomat in Swedish intelligence – tipped off the British naval attaché in Stockholm, Henry Denham.

It had now been only a few days since the Enigma code settings had arrived at Bletchley. Together with the papers from the weather ship *München,* Turing's team was now able to decode messages in just six hours. They had also found instructions for special message settings for officers only. As Joe Baker-Cresswell headed back towards Iceland in *Bulldog,* a special signal about Operation Primrose arrived from the First Sea Lord, Dudley Pound:

> "Hearty congratulations. The petals of your flower are of rare beauty."

Despite Tovey's claim that he just sat around, the message that the *Bismarck* may try to break out into the Atlantic had been long expected, and he put into effect the procedure that dated back to January, when a similar tip-off had been received from Törnberg that *Scharnhorst and Gneisenau* were leaving the Baltic. This had combined with being able to read Luftwaffe Enigma signals reporting on the ice conditions around Iceland. On that occasion, the two German battlecruisers – commanded by the German admiral Gunther Lutjens – had been allowed to escape. There was a glimpse for the cruiser *Naiad*, using a new ship-based radar system in a snowstorm south east of Iceland, but no more.

The German signals stations picked up *Naiad*'s report and were able to deduce that Tovey's Home Fleet was at sea in search of them, but that they had also lost the scent. For the next seven weeks, they eluded their pursuers, though twice they were forced to escape from an attack on a convoy by the presence of a British battleship. On 23 March, having sunk 22 ships, they arrived in Brest.

When it was clear that *Bismarck* was doing exercises in the Baltic, there was suddenly the terrifying prospect of a double break-out – the two battlecruisers from Brest at the same time as *Bismarck* and the heavy cruiser *Prinz Eugen* made it around Iceland. This was delayed, at least, by what turned out to be a virtually suicidal RAF torpedo raid on the port facilities in Brest which damaged *Gneisenau*. As it turned out, *Scharnhorst* was also suffering from engine problems. Even so *Bismarck*'s sister ship *Tirpitz* was finishing sea trials in the Baltic, and the prospect had only been put off. The two together would have been a match for the Home Fleet, even without spreading old battleships across the convoy routes.

Tovey was genial, stubborn and deeply religious. He was unsure which way around Iceland Lutjens would take his ships and was forced to divide his forces. *King George V* and the battlecruiser *Repulse* stayed with him, while Vice-Admiral Lancelot Holland took the new battleship *Prince of Wales* and the popular and famous battlecruiser *Hood* further west. On the evening of 23 May, the cruiser *Suffolk*, equipped with the new sea-going radar, sighted *Bismarck* and *Prinz Eugen* heading through the Denmark Strait. Holland's force was within striking distance, and they sped through the night to cut them off.

Tovey always kept radio silence at sea. Although neither he nor his superiors realised their signals were being read, he knew that the enemy could track his wireless signals and pinpoint his position. It made sense, therefore, to stay silent, though he was receiving signals from *Norfolk* and *Suffolk*, because Lutjens was only too aware of their presence and their position. At dawn, *Hood* and *Prince of Wales*, brand new and still with builders on board, were in position with high expectations, and it was then that disaster struck.

Hood had been designed before the Battle of Jutland in 1916 had revealed a serious flaw in the defences of the British battlecruisers, allowing shells to penetrate into the magazines where the explosive shells were kept, with disastrous results. Jutland had been a quarter of a century before, and the shock at the loss of three battlecruisers in quick succession had all but died down. But it was about to happen again. Only minutes before 6am, as Holland's squadron dashed into position, a shell from *Bismarck* penetrated *Hood's* magazine. There was a tremendous explosion and *Hood*'s famous profile disappeared, leaving only three survivors.

The horrified crew of *Prince of Wales* then received the full onslaught, taking a hit in the bridge. When one of the brand new turrets jammed, Captain John Leach decided to pull away behind a smokescreen. It was Empire Day, 24 May, and it had been a humiliating disaster for the British navy.

But the action had also been something of a shock for Lutjens. Although some kind of response from the British must have been likely, he had not realised that the Home Fleet had been at sea. There had been no reconnaissance flights over their base at Scapa Flow because of fog and the signal traffic had been silent. Now that he had seen the profile of *Prince of Wales*, he also believed they had been fighting her sister ship, the flagship *King George V*. Not long after the battle, confirmation came in: "Reported battleships still in harbour". The signal added "dummies are possible". As Lutjens knew very well, they certainly had been dummies. Tovey's fleet had been at sea and he had defeated it, or so he thought.

In fact, of course, Tovey *was* at sea but not there. He had a new battleship, but his battlecruiser was also of pre-1916 design and it seemed foolhardy to expose it in a second disastrous action. In his favour, before breaking off the action, *Prince of Wales* had scored three hits on *Bismarck*. These did not affect the ship's operational effectiveness but it now made sense for Lutjens to make for a port. Since he believed Tovey had been vanquished, it made sense to press on into the Atlantic. It was when Lutjens was told that the ship was probably *Prince of Wales* that he decided to make straight for Brest.

Norfolk and *Suffolk* reported that *Bismarck* was trailing oil. Tovey knew that there had must have been damage, but which way would Lutjens go? To make matters worse, in the fog early the next morning, *Bismarck* dodged the shadowing cruisers successfully and Tovey was now completely in the dark, keeping his own fleet between Lutjens' assumed position and the way north to Norway.

Churchill was apoplectic about the loss of *Hood*. All the resources of the Admiralty were behind Tovey. The battleship *Rodney*, on its way to the USA for much-needed repairs, was turned back in mid-Atlantic and ordered to join him. Force H, including the aircraft carrier *Ark Royal,* was heading north from Gibraltar. Denning at OIC was sleeping under his desk at the Admiralty's Citadel. Bletchley Park was hard at work decoding. The scene was set for a monstrous misunderstanding.

At the end of a tumultuous day, Bletchley's Hut 4 realised that *Bismarck*'s control station had shifted from Wilhelmshaven to Paris, the headquarters of the German navy's Group West. OIC understood that this strongly implied that Lutjens had turned south east. Believing that contact had not been lost with the shadowing cruisers, Lutjens also made the mistake early the next morning, of making a long signal to his own commanders. The Admiralty was unable to read the signal so soon but was able to plot the position it came from on a map, and it was again clear that Lutjens was heading south east. Unfortunately, the Admiralty did not pass this conclusion on, simply sending the map references – and doing so encoded in such a way that it confused Tovey's staff. They plotted the position wrongly on their own map on board *King George V* and concluded – wrongly again – that *Bismarck* was heading north.

For most of the day, the Admiralty watched Tovey's fleet steam north at speed, assuming that somehow he had access to better information than they did, or that the direction finders on board his destroyers were telling him something different. In fact, Tovey had sent his destroyers – including *Somali,* which had been accompanying *Rodney* – home to refuel.

**

Bletchley Park also had a clue about *Bismarck*'s direction. In Hut 6, where they decrypted Luftwaffe and army signals, they decoded a message from the chief of staff to the Luftwaffe general Hans Jeschonnek in Greece. It implied that a close relative of the general's was on board *Bismarck* and he wanted to know where it was going. Jeschonnek had no son himself, but it was clear he had a family interest in Lutjens' intentions. In answer, Luftwaffe command copied Lutjens' signal of early on 25 May, put it into Luftwaffe Enigma code and passed it on to Athens. Bletchley saw its significance immediately, but could not read the position or course.

Desperately, the cryptographers searched for the original naval signal in the piles of unread traffic. When they found it, they still could not read it. Then it dawned on them that the operator had made a mistake. They tested out a series of possible mistakes before one of them finally unlocked the message within. There was the *Bismarck*'s course and position set out in black and white. A Catalina flying boat was sent up to check early on the morning of May 26, and there was *Bismarck*, no longer with *Prinz Eugen*, heading desperately towards Brest and trailing oil as she went.

Just before Bletchley Park finally cracked the Luftwaffe signal, Tovey had realised something was going wrong. Why were ships being sent south when he was heading north as fast as he could? He signalled the Admiralty for instructions. All finally became clear, but it seemed likely to be too late. His ships were short of fuel and he could go south at speed only until the following morning (27 May) before he had to turn around. Something had to happen to slow *Bismarck* down.

Ark Royal made two attempts to attack with torpedoes, ordered by the colourful Force H commander Sir James Somerville. The first time, they attacked the shadowing cruiser *Sheffield* by mistake. The second time, late on the evening of 26 May, they believed there had been no hits. But there had been a hit: inexplicably, *Bismarck* began turning north, her rudder bent out of shape by an unlucky torpedo strike from the air. Aware from the decrypts of the fate that awaited him, Lutjens was also sending signals freely now, asking for more fuel. If they had not been leaking oil, they could have progressed faster and almost be under the air cover from Brest.

For the German navy, the signals were unbearable. It was clear that *King George V* and *Rodney* were now speeding as fast as they could towards the position where *Bismarck* was steaming slowly in a circle. Ten hours before they caught up, Lutjens received the following signal:

"To CinC afloat. I thank you in the name of the entire German people. Adolf Hitler. To the crew of the battleship Bismarck. All Germany is with you, all that can still be done, will be done. Your devotion to duty will fortify our people in their struggle for existence. Adolf Hitler."

This message was decrypted by Bletchley Park on 29 May. The truth was, not much could be done, though the Spanish were asked to send a cruiser to the scene to look for survivors, much to Hitler's rage. The final signal read:

> "Ship unmanageable. We shall fight to the last shell. Long live the Fuhrer."

It was a long wait for execution. Tovey's fleet arrived at dawn on 27 May and *Bismarck* was soon a floating wreck. Forced to break off the action through lack of fuel, Tovey ordered the cruiser *Dorsetshire* to finish her off with torpedoes. The *Bismarck's* survivors maintained later that they had scuttled her. The final message decoded from naval headquarters in Berlin read:

> "From Naval SE to GC and CS: Are bodies to be fished up?"

7

There were bodies to be fished up and exhausted, oil-covered survivors of the *Bismarck* to process and take back and into captivity. There is a famous photograph of them in the sea, trying to grab the ropes thrown down by the crew of the *Dorsetshire* to pull them to safety. A periscope was sighted shortly afterwards, so the rescue work was never completed, and – by the time the Spanish cruiser *Canarias* arrived on the scene – there was nothing to be found. A week later, the BBC European Service broadcast the names of the survivors on their German language channel, aware that listening to the BBC was punishable by the Nazis by death. By the end of the war, 15 million Germans were listening regularly.

By the end of the *Bismarck* episode, Bletchley Park had been able to use the information they had gleaned from the *München* and U110, and were able to decode the signals as they came in after a few hours. There would be periods of black-out again, when the German navy changed the basis of the codes – or added another rotor ring, and they eventually had a choice of eight – but this was the turning point.

From then on, once the bigram tables had been reconstructed, Turing's system would be brought into effect at the beginning of every month. Likely phrases would be recognised in signals and put through their 'bombe' prototype computers until one of these 'cribs' transformed coded gibberish into comprehensible German. But for the time being, Turing, Knox, Hinsley and their colleagues had the Enigma settings for naval forces in home waters for June and they were making the best of it.

As a result, between 1 and 23 June 1941, their ability to avoid U-boats by reading their position signals became so sophisticated that there were no attacks on convoys at all. In July and August, the tonnage sunk fell below 100,000 for first time for over a year. By November, it had dropped to 62,000, even though U-boat numbers had increased by half as much again (though some had also been sent to the Mediterranean).

It was too late to be able to apply this absolute mastery of German signals in June to the search for the *Bismarck*. She had been pursued and sunk with support from the cryptographers but the crucial information came from being able to read the Luftwaffe code not the naval one. *Prinz Eugen* was now on her way unmolested to Brest, which she reached on 31 May. But still at large in the Atlantic somewhere were the supply ships which had set sail with *Bismarck* from Gotenhafen and were now waiting fruitlessly to refuel and restock her bunkers. The old cruiser *Dunedin* and the aircraft carrier *Eagle* were constituted as Force F and sent south to seek them out. One signal suggested that a tanker would be waiting 900 miles west of the Canaries to refuel *Prinz Eugen* on June 2, and they were sent fruitlessly to find them.

The following day, another supply ship *Belchen* was scuttled when it was intercepted by the cruisers *Aurora* and *Kenya* in the middle of refuelling U93 off the coast of Greenland. The following day, the Enigma decrypts provided the material to catch *Gedania*, captured by the destroyer *Marsdale*, and the tanker *Esso Hamburg*, sunk by the cruiser *London*. The supply ship *Gonzenheim* was forced to sink herself by planes from the aircraft carrier *Victorious* and the sudden arrival of the battleship *Nelson*.

In fact, the capture of *Gedania* had been an accident. OIC had decided that to tackle so many supply ships on the same day would make the enemy suspicious that their codes had been compromised. *Marsdale* happened to surprise her unexpectedly.

The following day, 5 June, *London* and *Bulldog*'s sister ship *Brilliant* found the tanker *Ederland* and forced her to sink herself. The following day, planes form Force F found the supply ship *Elbe*, disguised as a Norwegian ship. Six days then passed before *Friedrich Breme* was sunk by *Sheffield*. That just left one of *Bismarck's* flotilla of supply ships left on the high seas. Where was *Lothringen*?

Again, it was the team at Bletchley Park which provided the answer. They took only four hours to decrypt a message ordering her to change procedures and to start supplying U-boats instead, and to make two rendezvous with four submarines on 17 and 18 June. On 14 June, another signal was decrypted, this time to the U-boats, describing *Lothringen* to them and warning them to "expect surprises". Clearly the German admiralty was nervous.

The following day at lunchtime, aircraft from *Eagle* sighted a tanker. They ordered it to stop but it ignored them. They hit the tanker with two bombs and set it on fire, and sent *Dunedin* south to finish the job.

Captain Richard Lovatt in *Dunedin* arrived at 5pm, nervous that *Lothringen* was still afloat, and had not been scuttled by its crew. Was there a U-boat lurking in the vicinity? He dropped depth charges on either side of the tanker to make sure this was no trap. A boarding party on board discovered *Lothringen*'s captain – from the merchant navy – and he agreed to hand over his ship if the wounded were looked after. Interviewing the crew later, it emerged there had been a titanic argument between the merchant navy captain and crew and the naval officers aboard. The chief engineer had refused to sabotage the engines on the grounds that he would only be forced to repair them again. It was not a happy ship.

Downstairs, the boarding party found that the code books had been destroyed and the radio operator had taken a sledgehammer to the wireless equipment. But behind the gramophone, they found a cipher log of all recent signals in plain language. Aware that this could be compared to the original signals in code, the boarding party packed it away. Lovatt decided the *Lothringen* should be sent to the docks in Bermuda. The final supply ship had been captured, and with the help of the Bletchley decrypts.

**

Bletchley decoded the distress signal from *Lothringen*, warning that they were under attack, but there was no reply from the German Group West naval command. Nor was there any warning to the U-boats due to rendezvous in a few days. The only conclusion they could draw was that German commanders had not received the original distress signal. They had not realised *Lothringen* had been captured. Bletchley Park contacted OIC with an urgent proposal. Why not make sure that *Lothringen* kept the four appointments with its new prize crew, and surprise and sink – and maybe capture – all four U-boats?

It could have been an extraordinary coup, but OIC weighed up the risk and refused. If any of the four rendezvous had gone wrong, it would have revealed that they had been able to read the signals which sent them to that position. Even if all four submarines had been captured and sunk, it would send a strong message that their signals had been compromised. No, Station X must be protected, the U-boats ignored and *Lothringen* must continue to Bermuda. The tanker was then reused by the British as *Empire Salvage*. *Dunedin* went onto capture three Vichy French merchant ships in the weeks that followed, finally sunk herself by U124 that November.

OIC's over-riding concern had been the protection of Bletchley's secrets, and it led to something of a paradox. The more they could read the signals, the less they could act on them – unless they could provide some other reason how the information was discovered. Too many accidents and coincidences and the enemy would suspect and change the way they organised Enigma. In particular, Dönitz would be even more suspicious than he already was. It was a delicate balance to shape. After all, if they made no use of the knowledge then all that effort to crack the Enigma codes would go to waste.

As it was, the settings were changing anyway. In the middle of June, U-boat command complicated matters even further by referring to areas of the Atlantic by new code names.

This was primarily designed to prevent information leaking out from the U-boat service to the rest of the German navy, which was the source that Dönitz most suspected. It took Knox and his team another month to pinpoint the new code words.

Meanwhile, the British cipher which B-Dienst knew as 'Cologne' was dropped altogether in 1942. Tranow's team cracked it again, assisted by the capture a few months later of a codebook for 'Munich' from the destroyer *Sikh*, sunk close into the shore during the Tobruk landings. British signals stayed virtually transparent, with gaps, thanks to B-Dienst, until June 1943 when the Anglo-American naval code – which B-Dienst called 'Frankfurt' – shifted onto a telex-based system. That then remained secure for the rest of the war.

Operation Primrose had been particularly important in the breaking of Enigma, and so the secret that U110 had been boarded and captured – however briefly – simply had to be defended. The main threat remained members of U110's crew in captivity, who were kept apart from each other as much as possible. Lemp's first officer Dietrich Loewe managed to talk to six former crew members, and none of them could swear they had actually seen their submarine actually sink.

One of the engineers was also given his citation for the iron cross back to him. It was possible, he told himself, that it had been in his overalls when he was captured. Equally, he had believed it had been in a folder in his locker. He told Otto Kretschmer, the former commander of U99 and Kretschmer decided to send a coded report to Dönitz.

The code had been developed for U-boat officers to communicate back home after they had been captured. It was very simple and based on morse code: the letters A to I represented a dot, J to R represented a dash and S to Z a space. In practice, you only really needed the letters I and R to be used in the first letters of a word embedded in a sentence in an ordinary letter home. Kretschmer used this code to send the message UE0, which meant simply that U110 was in enemy hands.

Nearly a year, in prison camp in Canada, Loewe met another member of crew said who had talked to others who confirmed they had seen U110 sink. He wrote another coded message: 'UE0 sunk, possibly enemy on board". Then in February 1944, he met another prisoner who confirmed that U110 had sunk. He sent the message "Boat sank. Nobody inside." It is hard not to suspect that these encounters were manipulated because Loewe was swapped for allied prisoners, perhaps in the hope that he might convince Dönitz in person that Enigma had never been captured or compromised, at least through U110.

**

Perhaps the most important question is the strategic one. There were talented, innovative and courageous people working on both sides of the struggle in naval intelligence. In Dönitz, the British faced a formidable, single-minded and determined mastermind who came close to starving the UK out of the war. The German side began the war with the great advantage that they could not just operate a guerrilla war at sea, but they could hear and read the signals sent by the other side. Why did one side survive and the other did not?

What seems to have been the British intelligence advantage was that, despite the conservatism and rivalry of the different armed forces, they were able to attract the mavericks who could work together effectively. They realised early on the critical importance of seeing the whole picture and organised systems which allowed them to get it, co-ordinating all the available information so that it poured into the Trade Mapping Room and the Submarine Mapping Room next door at the Admiralty.

What seems to have been the German intelligence disadvantage was that, suspicion being what it is in a totalitarian state, it was very hard to bring all this information together. Knowledge was power, and the mutual distrust between power centres meant that it was not pooled nearly enough. Dönitz's own suspicions focused first on his own navy, and his status as controller of a navy within a navy, 800 miles away in Lorient, may have been part of the problem.

Both sides were equally closed-minded about the possibility that their codes had been compromised. The British dismissed the coincidences as bad luck, when they should have been more sceptical. The Germans tended to dismissed similar setbacks in similar ways, or as an enemy within, espionage in headquarters. Both sides relied too much on their own invulnerability to cryptography. Dönitz asked difficult questions and his diary reveals how much he wrestled with this possibilities. But then again, his narrow focus allowed him to update codes in a way that the British navy simply could not, spread as they were across the globe.

It may also be that the ability of the Royal Navy to unbend was an advantage, to allow trusted mavericks and outsiders – like Alan Turing or Ian Fleming or Harry Hinsley – to play such key roles, was an important weapon, just as it is today. Informal structures have huge advantages over authoritarian ones. It means that brilliant amateurs are able to suggest wheezes, solutions and to challenge and cajole their senior officers. It may be that this was the most important advantage of all when intelligence was as important a factor as raw courage, and imagination as critical as seamanship.

There was no shortage of courage, seamanship or intelligence on either side in the Battle of the Atlantic, as the extraordinary casualty rate amongst U-boat crews and allied merchant seamen suggests. But informality has its place and, on this occasion, it really mattered.

Find out more

I am enormously grateful to the staff of the London Library for all their help, as always, with this book. It is the second short book I have written about submarines and the second about Enigma, and it was good – but complex – to bring the two stories together. By far the most important source, if you want to find out more, is Hugh Sebag-Montefiore's book *Enigma* (see below). There is now detailed information about the complexity of cracking naval Enigma, specifically in the pages put together by the former curator of the Bletchley Park museum, Tony Sale, at www.codesandciphers.org.uk. There are also a number of original documents about Operation Primrose at http://www.uboatarchive.net/U-110.htm Otherwise, I suggest consulting some of the following for aspects of this book.

Balme, D. (1993), 'Operation Primrose' in *Military History Journal,* South African Military History Society, Jun, Vol 9 No 3.

Batey, M. (2009), *Dilly: The man who broke Enigmas*, London: Dialogue.

Calvocoressi, P (1980), *Top Secret Ultra,* London: Cassell.

Gannon, J. (2001), *Stealing Secrets, Telling Lies,* Washington: Brassey.

Gill, S. (2003), *Blood in the Sea: HMS Dunedin and the Enigma code*, London: Weidenfeld and Nicolson.

Hinsley, F. H. (1951), *Hitler's Strategy*, Cambridge, CUP.

Hinsley, F. H. (1979), *British Intelligence in the Second World War,* London: Stationery Office.

Hinsley, F. H. (2001), *Codebreakers: The inside story of Bletchley Park,* new edtn, Oxford: OUP.

Hoyt, E. P. (1987), *U-boats: A pictorial history*, London: Staley Paul.

Kahn, D. (2000), *Hitler's Spies: German military intelligence in World War II*, New York: Da Capo.

Kennedy, L. (1975), *Pursuit: The sinking of the Bismarck*, London: Fontana Press.

Lenton, H. T. (1975), *German Warships of the Second World War*, London: Macdonald and Jane's.

Mallmann Showell, J. P. (2000), *Enigma U-boats: Breaking the* code, Shepperton: Ian Allan.

McLachlan, D. (1968), *Room 39: Naval intelligence in action 1939-45*, London: Weidenfeld and Nicolson.

Nesbit, R. C. (2008), *Ultra Versus U-boats: Enigma decrypts in the national archives,* Barnsley: Pen & Sword.

Richmond, J. (2002), 'Classics and Intelligence, Part II' in *Classics Ireland* Vol 9, 46-62.

Sebag-Montefiore, H. (2000), *Enigma: The battle for the code*, London: Weidenfeld and Nicolson.

Steury, D. P. (1987), 'Naval intelligence: The Atlantic campaign and the sinking of the Bismarck' in *Journal of Contemporary History,* Vol 22 No 2, Apr, 209-233.

Whitehouse, A. (1963), *Submarines and Submariners,* London: Frederick Muller.

Willmott, H. P. (2010), *The Last Century of Sea Power: From Washington to Tokyo, 1922–1945,* Bloomington: Indiana University Press.

Read the introduction to *Alan Turing: Unlocking the Enigma*

Published as an ebook by Endeavour Press, 2014, and as a printed paperback by the Real Press.

"Be it enacted by the Queen's most Excellent Majesty, by and with the advice and consent of the Lords Spiritual and Temporal, and Commons, in this present Parliament assembled, and by the authority of the same, as follows: 1 Statutory Pardon of Alan Mathison Turing."
Introduction to the draft law, introduced into the House of Lords, July 2013

It was unusually full for a Friday in the House of Lords as the peers gathered just before lunch on 19 July 2013. There, in the venerable red and gold of the Westminster debating chamber, Lord Sharkey – the former advertising executive John Sharkey – proposed a 'private members bill' to give a statutory pardon to one of Britain's greatest scientists, Alan Turing.

Present in the chamber to hear him were members of Turing's family, and at least one former colleague of his at the top secret code breaking establishment at Bletchley Park, where the Nazi Enigma code had been broken during the Second

World War. "Turing's reputation as one of the most brilliant scientists of the twentieth century has grown so much," said Sharkey, "that it now seemed extraordinary that he had been hounded for his homosexuality, and in the series of events leading to his suicide in 1954." More than half a century had gone by since those events, and it was time for the nation to make some amends.

The original campaign for a pardon was the idea of computer scientist John Graham-Cumming, who had begun by calling for an official apology for the way Turing was treated after his conviction. He wrote to the Queen to ask for Turing to be awarded a posthumous knighthood. The campaign won widespread support and, by 2009, Prime Minister Gordon Brown had agreed to apologise. "While Mr Turing was dealt with under the law of the time and we can't put the clock back, his treatment was of course utterly unfair," he wrote in the *Daily Telegraph*. "I am pleased to have the chance to say how deeply sorry I, and we all are, for what happened to him."

But the campaigners wanted more than just an apology; they wanted a proper pardon. The government refused on the grounds that it would set a precedent, even though pardons had recently been given to 18 former terrorists under the Northern Ireland Agreement and 304 of those shot for cowardice during the First World War. All that could be done, in the face of that refusal, was to change the law.

Sharkey was a Liberal Democrat peer and he had two interests in taking the campaign further. He had been campaigning for a blanket pardon for all the remaining 16,000 living victims of the Labouchère amendment to the Criminal

Law Amendment Act back in 1885, which had first criminalised homosexual acts, and tried to force the issue in Parliament in 2011. It gave pardons to all those still living who had been convicted, but it excluded those who had died, like Turing and another 59,000 people. Sharkey was advised that the best way forward to extend this would be to engineer a pardon for one of the very greatest of those convicted.

Sharkey's second interest was that he had always been a great admirer of Turing's, having studied maths at university under Robin Gandy, Turing's great friend and his only PhD student.

So the scene was set for an unusual event.

"My Lords," said Sharkey, rising to his feet. "On 6 August 1885, late at night in the Commons debate on the Criminal Law Amendment Act, Henry Labouchère suddenly produced an amendment to the Bill before the House. This amendment criminalised homosexual acts. The only discussion was over the penalty to be imposed. Labouchère had proposed a maximum of one year. Sir Henry James suggested two years and Labouchère agreed. The whole debate had four speakers, including Labouchère. It lasted four minutes and consisted of a total of 440 words, but 75,000 men were convicted under this amendment, and Alan Turing was one of those."

But it was already clear by then that, whether Sharkey succeeded or failed, Turing's reputation was rising all over the world, and he was increasingly prominent in so many of the most important debates of the early twenty-first century – about the nature of humanity, the possibilities of artificial life, the meaning of human endeavour, and the direction of 'progress'.

Turing had important things to say on all of these, and he is probably best known for his wartime code-cracking, but he ought perhaps to be better known for his pioneering contribution to the very beginning of information technology. Partly he had been overlooked until now because of a rivalry between the supporters of rival American and British claims to have originated computing, and partly it was because of the self-effacing personality of the man himself. It was also partly because of his early death, two weeks before his forty-second birthday.

But that is changing. Alan Turing appears to be becoming a symbol of the shift, not just towards computing but by his attitude of open-minded defiance of convention and conventional thinking. Not only did he conceptualise the modern computer – imagining a simple machine that could use different programmes – but he put his thinking into practice in the great code-breaking struggle with the Nazis in World War II, and followed it up with pioneering early work in the mathematics of biology and chaos.

As if that wasn't enough, he has now assumed the status of a martyr of the modern age, for his logic, his rationalism and his unashamed homosexuality, and for the way he was treated as a result by the forces of the law – and of course because this appears to have led to his suicide.

Turning himself, as one might expect, was a strange mixture of character traits and paradoxes. Confident in his own abilities, amusing and witty with friends, yet shy and uncertain in company, except with the few people he trusted. Relying on relentless logic, yet also managing an almost mystical ability to intuit mathematical proofs. He combined a rigid clarity and scepticism about human specialness, but he was also fascinated by fairy tales and was famously obsessed with the Disney film *Snow White and the Seven Dwarfs.*

The overwhelming feeling about Turing, reading the details of his life – and his mother wrote a detailed tribute after his death – is just how English he was. Many of his fellow countrymen failed to understand him at all, and he worked part of his career with American and German mathematicians at Princeton University, but he was deeply English in his sheer practicality, for the literalism with which he turned intellectual ideas into practical projects, and for his empiricism. He was a true successor to the great British empiricists, John Locke and David Hume, and the exclusion of every consideration except sense data. It is a theme that keeps returning in his life and work.

My own interest in Turing began when I was writing about the changing meaning of the word 'authenticity', and Turing was a particularly paradoxical figure in this debate. He remains the hero of those who believe that technology will rapidly replace the purely human. Yet there are elements of Turing's multi-faceted personality that it would be possible to hail on the other side – his belief in human possibility, his tolerance and above all his romanticism: one of his closest friends was the future fantasy writer Alan Garner, later the author of *The Weirdstone of Brisingamen.*

But I have always been interested in Turing for another reason too. He was born in the neighbourhood where I was brought up, a Georgian enclave near Paddington Station in

London, known for its plane trees, its dubious Edwardian night life and for its network of canals, earning it the title 'Little Venice'....

Read the introduction to *Unheard, Unseen: Submarine E14 and the Dardanelles*

Published as an ebook by Endeavour Press, 2014, and as a printed paperback by the Real Press.

You, the mothers, who sent their sons from far away countries, wipe away your tears; your sons are now lying in our bosom and are in peace. After having lost their lives on this land they have become our sons as well."
Kemal Atatürk, 1934

The Dardanelles in the early hours of 27 April 1915. Here Agamemnon and the Greeks landed for the attack on Troy. Here Xerxes had ordered the sea to be lashed for destroying his invasion bridges. Here Lord Byron swam against the Hellespont current.

Now it was the very portals of the Ottoman Empire for the crew of the British submarine E14, staring silently into the darkness from the small conning tower, eight feet above the waves. It meant mines, forts, searchlights and wire s
ubmarine nets. It meant a formidable current pouring fresh water over strange and unpredictable layers of salt water up the 38 mile passage from the Mediterranean to the Sea of Marmora,

and through one narrow point only three quarters of a mile wide. It meant undertaking possibly the longest dive ever contemplated in a submarine.

It also meant passing the wreckage of the submarines that had tried to pass that way in the days and weeks before, the French submarine *Saphir* and the British E15, lying wrecked and battered on a sandbank off Kephez Point, their dead buried on the beach, their survivors in captivity.

The sea was absolutely smooth and there was only a breath of air from the movement of the submarine itself. The canvas screens around the bridge had been removed to make the conning tower less visible. The electric batteries that would power their motors underwater had been charged to their highest pitch, as they waited in their harbour of Tenedos with its medieval castle, its windmills and its Greek sailing *caiques*, just a few miles from the site of ancient Troy.

E14 had weighed anchor at 1.40 in the morning. There was no escort for their lonely voyage. The goodbyes had been said. They had written their farewell letters, knowing that the chances were now against their survival, and given them into safekeeping.

The submarine's captain, Lieutenant Commander Courtney Boyle, had written three – to his wife, his parents and his solicitor – in the three hours warning he had been given at Mudros harbour the day before. Now he stood in his navy greatcoat, holding onto the rail, his binoculars around his neck, staring ahead in the blackness at the navigation lights of the allied warships, the greens and reds slipping away behind him. Next to him, his navigating officer, Lieutenant Reginald

Lawrence, only 22 years old, a reserve officer from the merchant navy, who had been there just a year before in peacetime. Below, the executive officer, Edward Stanley, was supervising the control room, listening to the rhythmic pulse of the engines.

It was a flat calm and there was no moon. From the northern shore in the distance ahead of them came the boom of guns and the flash of high explosive, a reminder that British, Australian, New Zealand and Indian troops were now dug in on the beaches, after their dramatic and perilous landings 48 hours before. Closer to the invasion beaches, they could see the shimmer of tiny glows from the trenches, the cigarette ends and makeshift fires of the soldiers dug into the dunes.

On their left hand side, there was a huge searchlight by the Suan Dere river; Boyle's first objective was to get as close as possible to the estuary there before diving. Beyond that, he could see searchlights on both shores, sweeping the sea ahead of them. He and Lawrence reckoned the one past the white cliffs on the southern shore must be Kephez Point, where E15 had come to grief and, further ahead, a more powerful yellow light, was the great fort at Chanak.

One diesel engine drove them ahead, and the noise and the fumes were horribly apparent to anyone on the conning tower, where the exhaust pipe was. Boyle was as experienced a submarine commander as any other afloat, but he was aware that he had not quite earned his commander's confidence. The calculations about speed, battery endurance, current and all the rest had been going through his head constantly since the dramatic meeting in the fleet flagship just two weeks before when– like all but one in the room – he had judged the venture impossible. That single dissenting voice was now dead.

He was aware also that, if the commander of E15 had not declared the passage of the Dardanelles possible by submarine, then almost certainly – as the most senior commander present – he would have been asked to try anyway. The one ray of hope was that the Australian submarine AE2, under the command of Henry Stoker, had now signalled that they had got through. This news had reached the E14 immediately before their departure and had changed the mood of the crew from resigned acceptance to hopeful elation. The passage of the Dardanelles must be possible after all, even if it remained extraordinarily hazardous.

But Boyle did have a plan. It was to get as far as possible to conserve their battery before diving, to dive as deep as possible under the obstructions, but to rise to periscope depth as often as possible in the most difficult sections of the journey, where the current was most unpredictable, to make sure the submarine did not drift He was acutely aware that his own skill and experience was now the determining factor, above all others, in his survival, the survival of the other 29 men on board, and of course of the success or otherwise of the mission.

They passed a brightly lit hospital ship, with its red crosses illuminated under spotlights, and then they were alone at the mouth of the Dardanelles. The crew were sent below and the engine room hatch was closed as a precaution. The Suan Dere searchlight loomed ahead, swept over them and then came back. Had they been seen? It flashed away again. It was clear from the experience of the ancient trawlers the British were using as minesweepers that the batteries ignored small ships on the way up the Dardanelles, waiting for them to drift closer to the shore as they turned back before firing. It was not clear either how much the stripped down conning tower was visible.

Then the searchlight was back and this time it stayed on them for 30 seconds. Lawrence gave a strained laugh. They had been seen. Boyle sent Lawrence below and ordered diving stations. By the time the hatch had been shut behind them, and they had swept down the iron ladder into the control room, two shots been fired. Lawrence settled down with his notebook in the control room. "Now we had really started on our long dive," he wrote later.

Everything now depended on the captain's skill and the resources of their electric batteries to drive them underwater...

David Boyle is a co-director of the New Weather Institute, and the author of a number of books about economics, business and the future, as well as history, including *Blondel's Song* and *Toward the Setting Sun*, about the discovery of America. He has written a series of successful titles for Endeavour Press, including *Unseen, Unheard: Submarine E14 and the Dardanelles* and the bestselling *Alan Turing: Unlocking the Enigma.* www.david-boyle.co.uk

Other titles by David Boyle

Building Futures
Funny Money: In search of alternative cash
The Sum of our Discontent
The Tyranny of Numbers
The Money Changers
Numbers (with Anita Roddick)
Authenticity: Brands, Fakes, Spin and the Lust for Real Life
Blondel's Song
Leaves the World to Darkness
News from Somewhere (*editor*)
Toward the Setting Sun
The New Economics: A Bigger Picture (with Andrew Simms)
Money Matters: Putting the eco into economics
The Wizard
The Little Money Book
Eminent Corporations (with Andrew Simms)
Voyages of Discovery
The Human Element
On the Eighth Day, God Created Allotments
The Age to Come
What if money grew on trees (*editor*)
Unheard, Unseen: Submarine E14 and the Dardanelles
Broke: How to survive the middle class crisis
Alan Turing: Unlocking the Enigma
Peace on Earth: The Christmas truce of 1914
Jerusalem: England's National Anthem
Give and Take (with Sarah Bird)

People Powered Prosperity (with Tony Greenham)
Rupert Brooke: England's Last Patriot
How to be English

Printed in Poland
by Amazon Fulfillment
Poland Sp. z o.o., Wrocław